PROFESSION:
IS CAREER YOUR CHOICE?:
A BOOK ON VEDIC ASTROLOGY

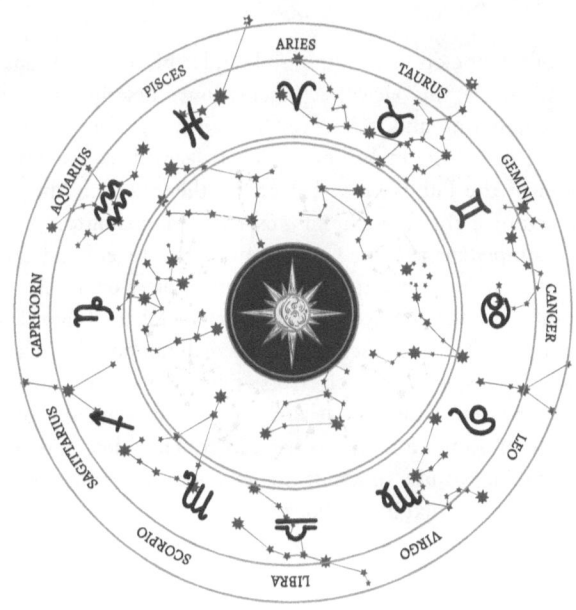

S NALLAKUTTALAM

Chennai • Bangalore

CLEVER FOX PUBLISHING
Chennai, India

Published by CLEVER FOX PUBLISHING 2023
Copyright © S NALLAKUTTALAM 2023

All Rights Reserved.
ISBN: 978-93-56487-25-3

This book has been published with all reasonable efforts taken to make the material error-free after the consent of the author. No part of this book shall be used, reproduced in any manner whatsoever without written permission from the author, except in the case of brief quotations embodied in critical articles and reviews.

The Author of this book is solely responsible and liable for its content including but not limited to the views, representations, descriptions, statements, information, opinions and references ["Content"]. The Content of this book shall not constitute or be construed or deemed to reflect the opinion or expression of the Publisher or Editor. Neither the Publisher nor Editor endorse or approve the Content of this book or guarantee the reliability, accuracy or completeness of the Content published herein and do not make any representations or warranties of any kind, express or implied, including but not limited to the implied warranties of merchantability, fitness for a particular purpose. The Publisher and Editor shall not be liable whatsoever for any errors, omissions, whether such errors or omissions result from negligence, accident, or any other cause or claims for loss or damages of any kind, including without limitation, indirect or consequential loss or damage arising out of use, inability to use, or about the reliability, accuracy or sufficiency of the information contained in this book.

CONTENTS

Preface .... *iv*

1. Is Career a Choice? 1
2. General Perspective - Livelihood/Career 6
3. Combination For Various Professions 15
4. Planetary Combination For Politics 46
5. Career In The Film Industry & Sporting Arena 58
6. Career And Foreign Settlement 70
7. Foundation-Education 81
8. The Important House 10th House 87
9. The Pivot (Dasamsa/D10) 95
10. Navamsa -D9 106
11. Importance of Planets In 10th House 114
12. Timing In Profession 126
13. Asthakavarga And Profession 131
14. Excerpts From Classical Text 136
15. Significator or Karaka 142
16. Significance of Planets And Income 148

Blurb *154*

PREFACE

Astrology is a study of the planetary position and its effect on the life of an individual. An astrologer, referred to as a Jyotish in the Indian context, knows how to read the birth chart correctly and helps an individual understand how life will be in the future. The work of an astrologer is to understand the planetary position and decode its effect.

People usually wonder about their life ahead. What is the correct career option for them, and if it would be the right option in the long run? Such curiosity is primarily seen in young people or by people looking for a change in career options as they stand at an uncertain juncture in their lives and need to decide and take a call about their upcoming days. As far as interest goes, people can have a variety of interests and passions.

However, not everything that interests' people can be taken as a career. Clarity regarding the position of the planets and their effect helps people make an informed decision on their career choices. A good astrologer studies the position of the planets and makes predictions, allowing people to know their personality type and the effect of their choices.

PREFACE

My interest in astrology started at the young age of 19. I started reading books written by different astrologers. Then I understood the effect of stars, the different kinds of personalities according to their planetary position and the different Zodiac signs. I started to learn the mysteries behind those charts and learnt to decode them. I understood the deeper meaning of birth charts, which only a learned astrologer could do. For the last few years, I have studied notable horoscopes to understand their unique and distinct features. I have shared a few horoscopes and explained the prediction to understand the readers better. The fact is there isn't a lot of good astrological work available in the area of profession and career, which prompted me to make up my mind to attempt this book titled *Is Career Your Choice?* The book analyses various combinations in the horoscopes and the timing of events as important factors.

I have made an earnest attempt to bring across a balance of concepts, rules, and excerpts from classical texts and added live examples to the core of the book. I have emphasized the usage of Varga charts, Asthakavarga and timing of events for the simple reason that some of these tools of Vedic astrology are not widely used anymore. This work is an outcome of little research, primarily on the combination of planets necessary for a particular profession. The book analyses the various combinations present in high-profile horoscopes.

This is my fourth book on astrology. My first three books were based on general perspectives on astrology. My new book touches on a niche subject which will arouse the readers' interest. Every student of astrology or anyone interested in understanding the concepts of astrology will thoroughly enjoy this book. It is an honest effort to enlighten my readers on the different perspectives of astrology to allow them to make an informed choice while choosing a career option. It is a chance to know yourself and your personality better and to take a peek into the future ahead. It gives you an idea about the turfs and valleys in the upcoming days of life. It will help people understand the kind of education and career they should go for and the kind of success and income that will come their way.

To understand your own birth chart or the astrological position and implication of the position of the stars, consult a Jyotish or an astrologer, or you can log on to our website, www.astrothoughts.in.

Leave your details and the kind of service you are looking for, and our team will get back to you at the earliest.

We will be eager to get feedback in any form from all my readers, which I am sure readers will love to share. It will enable me and my team members to do more creative work in the field of astrology in the years to come.

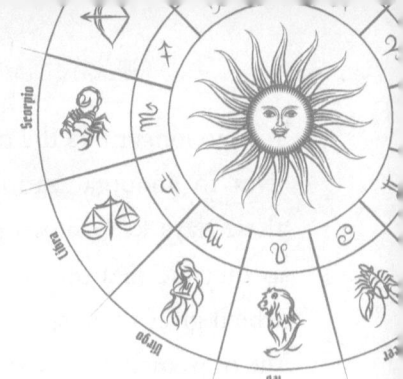

CHAPTER 1

IS CAREER A CHOICE?

What is a Career?

After years of education and internship courses comes the time when you are looking around to find yourself an opportunity to assign yourself a task where you commit time to an organization or institution that remunerates you for your effort. This time comes after years of waiting when you sign the documents and get assigned to a job. There are butterflies in your stomach, and you want to be sure you made the right decision. For most people, a career means a part of life concerning employment. Yes, this includes various employment opportunities they experience during their entire working lifespan. I simply understand a career as something people do to keep themselves employed. It may be for gainful purposes or with any other motive. It is better to look at careers in a more encompassing way. It can be viewed as the sum total of all decisions made for one's betterment encompassing the socio-economic environment.

It is no longer like the olden times when people gave their entire lives to an organization. The wanderlust career-seeking birds these days keep moving on from one assignment to the other as they are tied up to an organisation on a fixed-term contract, which gives them space to move on in life. However, along with the movement, every time, a thought recurs in your mind if you made the right decision regarding your career.

Career decision making

It is a world full of competition. So, each position advertised would have many aspirants. So, the decision-making is according to the available alternatives in the employment market. Normally, career decisions are a response mechanism to situations, problems, questions, etc., which aim to improve or achieve the desired value in life. Appropriate career decisions are life-long initiatives of choosing the right alternative, leading to a meaningful existence.

Career choices can spring from one's own thinking, behavioral pattern, liking for art or the compulsions of the society/community where one lives. These decisions are not always based on one's strengths and attributes, and there lies the problem. Either by one's own error in judgement or social compulsions, one can choose an inappropriate option, which has far-reaching effects at a later date in life.

Career decisions and age

Decision-making for young and mature adults differs. While the young usually move on the whims and fancies of the modern world. Adults weigh career prospects with a more mature perspective in which they look at currently available work and if it would have a future market for employment. However, regardless of the fact whether one is young or a mature adult, the basis for making such decisions remains the same. It is a reality that most of us are mature in thought with our age by life experiences which help us in the decision-making process.

These days, career counseling sessions are available in which people adopt different ways and mean to understand their own self. They use different strategies for different age groups of people. They believe that environmental scanning and understanding one's strengths and weaknesses differ with a person's age.

Culture and career choice

What is culture? In any society, there are accepted practices. These practices, over a period of time, become a way of life. This way of life is called and understood as culture. Over a period of time, culture changes. We find changes in the general perception of life, career choices, technology, fashion preferences, etc. Definitely, when an individual wants to decide on a career, the following factors come into play. Culture plays a vital role in career choice. There are many career choices which are readily accepted in some parts of the world. However, they will not be accepted in the world we exist in. It is due to the cultural difference. A choice of career is also based on the acceptability of the external environment which prevails around you.

a. Extrinsic factors

Extrinsic factors revolve around the benefits attributed to certain kinds of professions and also the regulations prevailing in the state.

Consequently, a person with "extrinsically factor motivation" may decide on a career or profession depending on its benefits. Most youngsters are motivated by the kind of lifestyle a career option might provide you and the kind of money it would fetch for the individual.

b. Interpersonal Factors

The influence of family, peer groups and teachers also go a long way in career decisions. People are sometimes coerced into taking career options, which is perhaps not their first choice in life. The preference of family, teachers and friends overrides the choice, undermining an individual's personal choice. It is a family or the culture of a society which gives weightage to the views of elders and people in the friend circle while taking a rational decision. Therefore, it is evident that culture plays an important role in career decisions.

The Dilemma!!

Now, we assume that an individual undergoes the above processes and decides on a career. Whether the individual will get his choice of profession or career is a mute question. In reality, the vast majority of people do not get what they want. Instead, they settle down for whatever comes their way at the needy time in one's life. This is where the relevance of astrological intervention comes in.

Classical astrological works were written long ago and have to be interpreted appropriately and put to use in the present day. The various astrological works point out the skill set, its application and available environment for an individual to make appropriate career decisions.

In this book, an attempt has been made to see what rules will throw light on career choices, career success and individual growth. Since most known astrological works are dated to the last few centuries, we will twig it to better understand the intended choice process and its success. It will be interesting to know the various indicators that astrological studies bring into play. After reading this book, you will understand that an experienced astrologer will be of great value as a counsellor for making career choices and making amends or changes at the appropriate time.

The readers will stand to benefit from the knowledge shared in the book, which will explain why certain people make certain choices in life and what impact it would have in their lives in the long run.

CHAPTER 2

GENERAL PERSPECTIVE - LIVELIHOOD/CAREER

General Perception of Career

As you watch the night sky lying on your back, you look at its glitter and the star-studded celestial sphere. It looks as if there are diamonds embedded in a dark, velvety cloth. People can gaze at such beauty for hours together and feel the blessed moment of being alive. Unaware, the human mind hardly knows the effect of these astronomical giants in your life. Every aspect of your life's journey is affected by their presence. Your personal attributes, the kind of life you would lead, your interest areas, your career choices, your choice of partner and the kind of health and wealth factors which would influence your overall journey of life.

A career is a very important decision in life. Our career defines our personality and also shapes the overall path to our economic freedom. People are known by their occupation, which becomes part of their overall personality. When people are looking for career choices, people look for career guidance from people established in their field or even counsellors. However, another perspective on career needs to be explored while exploring your career choices. Astrology is a less explored aspect while making career decisions, which people should consult before finalizing their career path. It might help you choose what is meant according to the position of the stars and the time of birth.

Before we start the book, we will look at what links astrology has with career and livelihood. Many times, aspirations and desires of people in terms of career are not met in their lives. This may be due to many reasons. Even people with very good academic backgrounds and wealth cannot pursue a meaningful career. At this juncture, it is pertinent to point out that the previous birth Karmas play a pivotal role in aligning one's career. Astrology can be a reliable source for identifying one's career choices, changes in career and growth prospects.

At the start of the book, we have shared with our readers a general perspective about the astrological phenomenon and the available career options. How can you find out from your chart or horoscope your preferred career choices that you can make for your future? As you read the paragraphs, you will be able to gather a better understanding of the subject. Once you have a general perspective, you may go into the details to understand how the various aspects of astrological teachings lead us to a better career.

Astrology Helps with Career Choices

According to Steven Forrest, "Astrology is just a finger-pointing at reality."

A career is a job or jobs which people do to earn a living for themselves. People usually look at the current trend of jobs available in the market and their interest area before they take it. However, people are forced to think about the right career options either right at the start of choosing an option or when they come across an obstacle in their career path.

A career is what one actually does for one's livelihood. In Vedic Astrology, we can identify the skill set of any native that will move him towards success. People get interested in the career they want to pursue to earn their livelihood. A career path depends on one's Karma, which the 10th House denotes e in horoscopes. The 2nd and 11th Lord will indicate income generation. The 6th House Lord indicates the wellbeing and employment situation. We often come across several combinations and placements of planets which will lead to a job/profession/business. There would be subtle changes for these three types of careers.

Vedic Astrology was written somewhere in the year 5000 B.C. and has been in practice ever since. If people of the modern world create an understanding of the subject and learn to decipher the words written in Sanskrit, their understanding of the subject would increase so many folds. The epic stands relevant even in today's modern world. The classical texts of astrology, which were written by scholars centuries ago, the predictions based on that can be used for modern-day society, which needs to be tweaked. It all depends on the individual to choose a career based on the opportunities, skill sets and destiny. Destiny has a role to play, as quite a few individuals will not be able to pursue the career they want due to the influence of the position of the stars. Planetary influence has a role in fulfilling one's desires, which we will read and understand in the latter half of the book.

Important Houses

The foundation of people's life is based on the 12 zodiac signs. The entire birth chart is divided into 12 sections, forming a 360-degree, which is important for making predictions. Earlier in the book, I spoke about the importance of the 10th and the 6th house.

We have also discussed the significance of each of the 12 houses and the planets they occupy. However, it is pertinent to examine the following:

1. Status of the 10th and 6th Lord
    a) Whether they are well placed in their own house- Moolatrikonam or exaltation
    b) Associated by means of being conjunct or aspects
    c) Placement of 6th and 10th Lord in Kendra and Konas
    d) Karaka of the planets, i.e., 6th and 10th and the nature of the house they are placed
    e) Since Saturn is the planet of Karma, his status needs to be analysed
    f) Equally important are running Dasa/Bhukthi and transit
2. Good and bad times in one's career

a) If the planet associated with the 10th Lord and 6th Lord is weak, then the career in such an event will have ups and downs, and upheavals can be seen in the career path.
b) If the 10th House Lord is retrograde, predict job change in their career.

The classical text indicates the nature of career, technical competency, talent, skill sets and relationship with people in its own way. The astrologer has to link it up with modern-day requirements and tweak the information, which makes it befitting for modern readers.

Income Generation

The status of 11th, 2nd, 3rd and 5th Houses and its Lords have to be accounted for:

2nd	Income Generation
3rd	Communication, Perseverance
5th	Intelligence and business acumen
11th	Desires (or) aspirations

The strength of these planets and Dasamsa will play an important role in sustaining a good career.

Example Chart 1

	Venus Sun Ketu Mercury	Mars	
	Rasi		
			Jupiter
Moon	Sat Asc	Rahu	

This is the horoscope of an industrialist from an outstanding industrial family. Let us examine the planetary placement, conjunction, aspects and other important relationships. The horoscope indicates the individual's hard-working nature, strategic thinking, confidence and humility. Apart from his inherited wealth, he has built a business empire with strong fundamentals and values.

The placement of the 4th Lord Saturn in Lagna makes him hard-working, disciplinarian and humble. The placement of Lord at the 2nd and 5th House, being a first-rate benefic, in the 10th aspect, 2nd and 4th, and 6th is an excellent arrangement for success in business. All four placements in the 6th House enjoy the aspects of Jupiter with the Sun in an exalted position. This gives the person in discussion the resilience and strength to handle adversaries effectively. The latter part of his life brought him more laurels and success. The 12th Lord aspect in the 12th House makes him generous and philanthropic.

Chart 2

Saturn		Ketu	
Mars	Rasi		
Jupiter			
Venus Mercury Sun Asc	Rahu	Moon	

The native was the chairperson of one of the biggest industrial organizations in the country. The family ran a trust, showing their philanthropic side and their care for society. Lagna has Mercury, Sun, and Venus's conjunct, which are Lords of 9th, 10th and 11th House. This powerful combination makes him a master of wealth, broad outlook, strategic thinking and magnanimity.

An exchange between Lords of the 2nd and 4th House resulting in Lagna Lords getting Neechabhanga is an excellent position for success in generating income for the organisation and for himself. During his time, he built a business empire, fulfilling the aspirations and expectations of various stakeholders in the family and people associated with him and society.

Chart 3

Asc		Saturn Venus	Sun
	Rasi		Ketu Mars Mercury Moon
Rahu			
Jupiter			

The individual is the CEO of one of the biggest conglomerates in the world. Lagna Lord and 10th Lord Jupiter in its own House is an excellent place to work from. He is a self-made man. Another first-rate benefic is Mars getting Neechabhanga Yoga to generate considerable income for him and the stakeholders associated with him. 3rd House Lord is in its own House, making him an excellent communicator and a person with lots of tenacity. The 5th House Lord in his own House was a person with strong intellect and an excellent thinking process.

All the 3 horoscopes depict the role of the 10th, 6th, 2nd and 11th Houses, which have helped elevate the individual to a high position in the organisation and the society at large.

After the above-discussed example, it will be clear in your mind that the different Houses in your birth chart depict the story of how your career life will look. There is a lot of confusion in people's minds when it comes to career choices, and with the guidance of an astrologer, an individual can think wisely and make rational choices rather than picking options on whims and fancies. An astrologer can read your chart, tell you your strong attributes, and help you decide accordingly. People can save their energy and start on the right foot at the right time.

CHAPTER 3

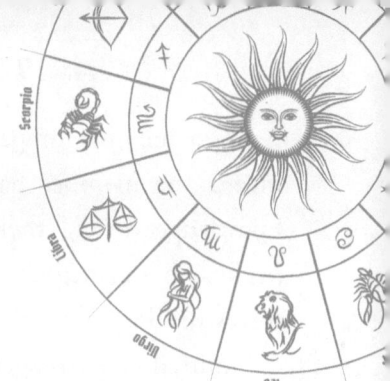

COMBINATION FOR VARIOUS PROFESSIONS

*A*fter taking a certain professional career, people study for years together to gain professional expertise in a certain subject. Once the degree is taken, people move for industry experience, usually short-term exposure in their specialty or interest. Now, the professional is ready to step into the heat of work where he gains industry experience and hones his skill set to serve a particular role.

Profession generally has three basic indicators. Professionals are people who have:

- Put in long years of studies in a particular field (expertise)
- Who profess ethical and moral standards
- They need not be supervised

Being a member or part of a profession or professional body means the member has integrity, ethics, trust, expertise and knowledge during their work conduct and also upholds the profession's principles, laws and conventions. A professional serves his duty not only for his own personal interest but is also committed towards society's larger good, which is a part of his moral and ethical values.

Astrological Outlook

From the astrological perspective, career prediction is according to an individual's planetary position and the zodiac sign at the time of their birth. The charts show an individual's inclination towards any particular activity and their personality type, briefly explaining the values they would uphold in life. Bhava, or the houses as expressed in Sanskrit, expresses the native of the individual, their behavior, heath characteristics, education, the wealth they would earn in their lifetime, family life and other characteristics which define various other attributes of a person's life. The 12 Bhavas of a chart reflects the various aspects of one's life.

The 2nd Bhava, or the **Dhana Bhava,** according to Vedic astrology, indicates income generation and wealth creation. When an astrologer studies the 2nd Bhava, it uncovers the material possessions an individual would acquire in his lifetime. This bhava also examines how a person values his material belongings and themselves. It also gives a brief look into the emotional side of the individual.

The profession that a person would take up is indicated in the 10th Bhava. It shows the means of livelihood which the person would take up at a later date. The honour and dignity a person would earn from his profession is part of the 10th bhava. Therefore, the 10th Bhava indicates the execution of actual work.

The 6th stands for success in job/employment, being the 9th from the 10th Lord. The 11th is the fulfilment of aspirations, desires and material gains for worldly success. There is a myriad of combinations for a successful professional. There will be benefic Yogas as well as Dosha depending on the placement, conjunction and aspect of planets in the Rasi and Varga Charts.

It will be a disastrous and stressful life if one chooses an inappropriate profession. The career choices can be best ascertained by reading the horoscope/chart. When people especially have choices, it is best to consult an astrologer. The timing of events will depend on Dasa and the prevailing Gochara, which will be dealt with in a separate chapter elsewhere in this book.

The results of major planets like Saturn, Jupiter, Sun, Rahu and Ketu will be profound in transit. Major Dasas for career progression will be Jupiter, Saturn, Sun and Mars. Quite a lot of information is available in the 10th Bhava, with considerable indicators from the 2nd, 6th, 9th and 11th Bhavas.

In our limited discussion, it may be impossible to cover the entire gamut of professions and services available in the market. We will now look at what kind of planetary arrangements will be present for different professions like:

a) Government Services (Elite)
b) A Medical Practitioner
c) A Lawyer and Judiciary functionary
d) An Engineer/Scientist

a) Government Services:

The important planets for government services are the Sun and Moon. If connected with the 10th House or 10th Lord, the twin royal planets can bring about a promising service. Normally, the strongest 10th House from (a) Lagna, (b) Moon, and (c) Sun can indicate what is in store for the native in government service.

Many desire to get employed within the government. Lakhs of people take up competitive exams to join government services. If academic performance is the only criterion, then all the university toppers would end up in government service. In reality, many top performers in universities fail to make it to the elite government services. If the astrological charts indicate a government service, then one can seriously try it out.

Some of the key take away indicators for government services are:

1. An association of the Sun and Moon with the Lords of 10th, 2nd, 9th and 6th
2. As per Jaimini Astrology, if the Sun is Amatya Karaka planet, then it strongly indicates a government job.
3. Saturn, the planet of masses, plays an important role in government service. A Saturn with dignity and strength in the horoscope will give an opportunity to serve the government and, thereby, the common people. Saturn's role is important for progress in any career.

4. If it is a uniformed service, be it military, police, etc., we will need a strong Mars for support.
5. We will need a well-placed Jupiter for judiciary, education and endowment boards.
6. The 6th House represents a service/job/employment. A strong 6th House will indicate a successful career.
7. According to Bhavat Bhavam, the 11th House becomes the 2nd House for the 10th House. Therefore, the 11th also gains importance.
8. A 5th and 9th House connection for the Sun and Moon augurs well for services.
9. Movable sign Aries, fixed sign Leo and common sign Sagittarius connections are strong indications for government service. These three signs indicate effective administrative and managerial skills.
10. Lagna Lord should be strong, and placement in 1st, 9th, 10th and 11th will be desirable.
11. A conjunction of the 10th Lord with the Sun, Saturn, and Jupiter in a beneficial Bhava will be welcome.
12. Prominent Raja Yogas, if formed as Dhana Yoga when present in the horoscope, will empower the native, for example, Pancha Maha Purusha Yoga, Gajakesari Yoga, etc.
13. The Varga Chart, especially Dasamsa, should be promising. We have discussed Dasamsa elsewhere in the book in detail.
14. Asthakavarga should have more bindus (or) points in the 1st, 6th, 9th, 10th and 11th Houses.
15. Shadbala should be more than the requested percentage. If 100% is a satisfying level, the planets responsible should have more strength than 100%.

16. It is desirable for the 10th and 9th Lord to be connected. An exchange between the 10th and 9th Lord goes with the name Dharma Karmathypathi Yogam.
17. Conjunctions between Jupiter and the Sun are highly desirable.
18. Saturn and Mars indicate machinery, travelling and chemicals. For railways, Saturn, Moon and Mars trio make it up.
19. Mercury comes into play in accounts and audit offices.
20. Favorable Dasa should be running, and the native will enjoy promotions and favorable transfers with advantageous transit (or) Gochara.

Example Chart 1

Being a civil servant is the dream of many people. Being a top officer in the government body and serving the high offices has a separate charm. It is a position of power, and people get a lot of fame and recognition by just competing in the exam. People serving in the position are strong administrators. People in these positions have a strong sense of legality and take up the liability of their actions and reactions to situations. They are usually hard-working and committed towards their job and use an out-of-the-box approach to sort situations and issues. They are decisive and resilient in approach and work on the principles of justice. They are usually good leaders, knowledgeable and have great communication skills. A unique placement of stars signifies the birth chart of a civil servant.

This is a chart of an elite civil servant who climbed the ladder to reach the very top. The native is known for his philanthropy and for his scholarly work.

	Mer Sun Venus Ketu	Moon	Mars
			Asc
	Rasi		Jupiter
	Saturn	Rahu	

One can see the exalted Lagna Lord Moon in the 11th House, which is unique. It is a planetary situation which is indicative of hope and the financial position of their employer. People with unique positions need the love and support of their loved ones all through their lives. These people get a lot of satisfaction with involvement in public service, with social organisation and their involvement in public life. That summarizes the entire story of the native's rise to dizzy heights in the elite service. The 2nd Lord is exalted in the 10th with 3 other planets, making the 10th House strong. There is an exchange between the 10th and 12th Lord, which is good for a Government servant. The 12th place and its Lord determine the service to the masses. The 10th House is aspected by Jupiter, which in turn makes the native vibrant and God-fearing.

Shadbala of the Sun is 213% and that of Jupiter 135% and is in an excellent position. Both the planets are rendered strong and effective, which will bring the government's support to the natives. The Moon, Jupiter, Venus and Ketu are in Pushkara Navamsa, making these planets resilient and strong.

Asthakavarga of the Lagna is 30, 2nd is 26, 6th is 29, 9th is 31, and 10th is 30, which is well above the required numbers. Overall, it is an excellent horoscope, true to it the native who reached the highest level of the elite service.

Example Chart 2

	Venus	Asc	Mars
Mer Sun Ketu	Rasi		
Jupiter Saturn Moon			Rahu

Most of us look forward to a government job for the simple reason that it comes with a lot of hard work, and the prestige attached to such jobs in all societies is huge. However, not all rise to such heights as there are a few planetary positions necessary for a person to reach such a position. People usually feel it is a place for university rank holders. However, we might find even a rank holder leading a very ordinary life. People working in these positions have the following traits and attributes.

Since it is a position which might have public interaction, people need to be honest and should have the humility to interact with people at large. They are usually open to learning through their experience, are extroverts and are not shy about expressing their views. They are considerate and emotional, making them a perfect fit for their position.

Above is a chart of a government servant whose planetary position is discussed below. This native rose to the highest possible position in a government of India Undertaking. Look at the first-rate benefic—9th and 10th Lord in its own House making a Sasa Yoga. The association of Saturn with Jupiter and Moon makes him the leader of the masses. Lakhs of people are dependent on the organisation, and the native takes care of them.

The 6th House is aspected by the 6th Lord, which means well for the chart indicating a strong job profile. The 10th House has the Sun and Mercury forming Budha Aditya Nipuna Yoga, which is an excellent combination. Look at the Shadbala of the following concerned planets:

Sun	191%
Saturn	135%
Venus	123%

This indicates the strength of the planets and, in turn, the chart. Rahu Dasa gave him employment and took him across the country for the next 18 years. From Jupiter Dasa in 2001, the native catapulted to senior positions.

In the Saturn/Venus period, the native became the chief of the organisation. The Asthakavarga is also promising.

House	Bindus
Lagna	25
2nd	30
6th	30
9th	29
10th	30

This is an excellent arrangement, and he has also received an extension in service.

b) A Medical Practitioner

Many children aspire to become a doctor right from their childhood. Children can be seen wearing a doctor's coat as a child playing games with their friends. However, there are only a few whose dreams translate into reality. As people grow, they see the prestige attached to the profession and the money that comes along with it. People attached to this profession are empathetic and show compassion towards people who are sick and suffering. They are good at observation and are good at multitasking. They are usually good communicators and are usually active people.

It is not only a noble profession but also a money spinner. The most intelligent and the most coveted choose this profession. It needs long years of studying for specialty and super specialty branches. The important aspects to look for are:

- The important Houses to be screened are 5th, 9th and 10th. The 1st, 5th and 9th Houses indicate higher studies and, especially, the 9th House for specialty branches. All these three Bhavas (or Houses need to be strong. Needless to add, the Lords of the 5th, 9th and 1st should have dignity and be well placed. The 10th House brings out the execution part and, therefore, gains significance.

The 2nd and 11th House and their Lords should be well placed since they indicate income generation and wealth creation. Only when a doctor prospers will he continue to excel.

- Amongst Rasi, Cancer, Scorpio and Capricorn would be important. For all three Rasi's, Mars is important, and it plays a vital role in the success of a doctor (or) paramedic.
- The planetary positions of Mars, Saturn and the Sun assume importance, and Mars plays a vital role in surgeries. If one is pursuing medicine, then Venus plays an important role.
- Mars and Saturn, well-placed in Kendras with dignity, assure the native to be a successful surgeon.
- When the 10th Lord in Navamsa is in Aries (or) Scorpio, then one becomes an effective surgeon.

- Mercury in Sagittarius on the 10th House will make one a successful doctor. But the Dasa of Mercury will not be a positive one.
- 10th Lord from Lagna, Sun or Moon occupying the Navamsa of Aries or
- Scorpio will enable one to become a doctor.
- The 2nd Lord occupying the 7th will make one an able hospital administrator and a qualified doctor.
- We will also see some of the common indicators which would lead to the medical profession.
- A conjunction of Sun and Saturn in any House which is beneficial from Lagna point of view
- Saturn aspecting the Sun
- Sun occupying Capricorn or Aquarius with strong Saturn
- Sun and Saturn in mutual Kendras to each other, i.e., 1st, 4th, 7th and 10th Houses are welcome.
- Venus in Capricorn or Aquarius, aspected by a strong Saturn, will make one a doctor of medicine
- The exchange between the 9th and 12th Lord indicates selfless service.
- Association between 8th and 12th Lord causing Vipareeta Raja Yoga.
- If one is employed, then a strong 6th house will have connections with 10th House.
- The Lord of the 5th house or 10th house is associated with the Lord of the 6th house. Then, one becomes an eminent doctor.
- Jupiter should be placed in 1st, 5th, 9th or 10th for upholding the ethics.

- Conjunctions of the following combinations in 1,5,9,10, and 11 would lead to the rise of a successful doctor.
- Sun, Moon, Mercury
- Sun, Moon, Venus
- Sun, Mercury, Jupiter
- Moon, Jupiter, Venus
- Moon, Mercury, Jupiter

Example Chart 3

Mars plays an important role in the life of a surgeon. Not all doctors become surgeons. A surgeon needs to be a good academician beyond all requirements. It is years of undeterred study and practice which gives shape to the skilled hands of a surgeon. A surgeon is a good communicator and a keen observer. However, once they reach for surgery, people are not in their best mental shape. So, a surgeon also balances situations and multitasks to take people back to health. Planets like the Sun, Jupiter and Moon play a significant role in the life of a surgeon. Below is the horoscope of a leading thoracic surgeon/medicine who excelled in practice and had academic brilliance.

	Ketu		
Moon	Rasi		
Saturn		Asc Venus Rahu	Sun Mars Mercury Jupiter

There are several indicators in this Chart to prove the native's success:

a) Association of Sun and Mars in the 12th
b) 9th and 12th Lord in exaltation, that too in the 12th House
c) Lagna Lord and 10th Lord in Kendras
d) 10th Lord aspecting the 10th House, which is definitely a blessing
e) The association of Rahu with Venus and the period of Rahu is very productive
f) Conjunctions of Sun, Mercury and Jupiter in the 12th House
g) Aspect of Jupiter on 10th Lord. This aspect will enable the native to have ethical conduct.
h) Asthakavarga points are good and above 28 in the 1st, 9th and 10th Houses.
i) Shadbala of Venus, Moon and Mercury are above 100%, which augurs well for the native to become an effective doctor.

Example Chart 4

			Ketu
	Rasi		Jupiter
Moon			
Mars Rahu Asc	Venus	Saturn Mer	Sun

When the Sun, Saturn, Moon and Jupiter have a connection with the 1st, 2nd, 10th and 11th house and their lords, a person is said to be a successful doctor.

This is a horoscope of a leading doctor of medicine. Venus plays a major role in the life of a doctor who practices medicine. The doctor had a thriving practice with great medical acumen. He was also a philanthropist and man of service to the poor and needy.

- Lagna Lord exalted in the 8th forming Gajakesari Yoga, which is beneficial and makes the native strong with lots of energy
- 5th Lord Mars in Lagna with Rahu with utmost dignity, which shows him with healing capacity
- 2nd Lord exalted in the 11th, which augurs well for income generation and wealth creation

- 10th Lord, in association with Saturn, a friend and also in a friendly sign, will make it stronger. It will enable the native to build a healthy professional acumen
- Started practice in the period of Rahu, which is in association with Lagna Lord in Lagna itself.
- A very promising start around the age of 39, Jupiter Dasa started which was a runaway success
- The Shadbala percentage of planets is as follows:

Sun	Saturn	Mercury	Rahu	Jupiter	Moon
166	140	119	141	127	110

It indicates the excellent dignity of all the planets involved, which took the native to dizzy heights in his profession.
- Additional information is that Mars, Venus and Ketu are in Pushkara Navamsa, which renders the planets strong and effective.

I hope these two examples will be sufficient. The more we look at this, the more we will be convinced about our thinking.

c) A Lawyer and Judiciary Functionary

Everyone has aspirations, dreams and desires with regard to their career/profession. For a person to function as a lawyer, the individual needs to have a deep understanding of the subjects in question and be a great communicator. The person needs to be a voracious reader to read the books of law and have critical thinking to analyse the different perspectives. The person should be a knowledge seeker. So, he needs to have the qualities of a researcher. With the help of this, he can prepare different strategies for cases. The job of a lawyer is that of perseverance and creativity, where he looks into different cases with a new perspective. Logical thinking and the power to express logically are strong traits of a person practicing law. Rahu is the planet which helps a lawyer in the process of discussion and arguments. When the Moon and Venus are in the same house, and one of the planets is in a higher position, the chances of a person being a successful lawyer are very high.

Now, let us discuss the various planetary arrangements for a successful career in law or judiciary. It is one of the commendable and prestigious professions. A large number of students clear law graduation every year, but only very few succeed in their profession. Getting into brass tacks, we find the following:

a) Mercury, Venus, Jupiter and Rahu have a distinct role in the field of law.
b) If Rahu is related to Mercury and has a 6th House connection, then we can predict a successful lawyer.
c) A combination of Mercury and Venus with dignity ensures a successful career in law.
d) If Mars is in Aries, Leo, Scorpio and Capricorn in the 1st, 9th and 10th House, then it will give rise to an excellent lawyer.
e) There will be positive vibes if there is a combination of Moon and Jupiter, like Gajakesari Yoga in the Lagna, 5th, 9th and 10th.

- If one needs to be a judge, then the role of Jupiter comes into play. The following combo brings in an effective judge: Saturn, Mars, Jupiter and Sun.
- Mercury, Jupiter, and Mars are in the 9th or 10th House.

- Jupiter in Sagittarius, Pisces and Cancer in Kendra (1,4,7,10) or Kona (5,9), then the native becomes an eminent judge.
- The 2nd House is for communication, and it should be strong. Benefics (or) functional benefics occupy the 2nd House, and then the native's verdict will be remembered.
- The 6th is the House of Litigation, and if associated with Rahu/Ketu, it can give rise to a judge/magistrate.
- An aspect of Jupiter to the 6th House enhances one's proficiency as a judge.
- The 9th House is related to the judiciary, and it needs to be fortified. Benefics occupying (or) aspecting will enhance the powers of the 9th House.
- The 10th House is the actual House of profession and should be strong with the 10th Lord having dignity. Benefics occupying the 10th House identical to their own house (or) well-placed malefic will make the person hard-working with integrity. Ashthagavarka points and Shadbala of the 10th Lord, if strong,
- will take the native to high positions in the judiciary.
- Sun also plays a vital role in a government job. So, for elevation in a judiciary career, Sun has to be placed well with dignity. Sun in the 10th House is welcome.
- Saturn is the planet of law and ensures the rendering of justice to the masses.
- Saturn, if well placed with 6th & 10th House connections, can take the
- native to name and fame.
- Rahu is important for diplomacy.
- Rajyogas present in Kendras (1,4,7 and 10) and Konas (5,9), and mutual aspects of these planets will make a Lawyer or Judge more balanced in outlook.

- Budha-Aditya Yoga makes a lawyer clever, communicative and intelligent in arguments.
- If a dignified Mercury is associated with the 10th House, one becomes a corporate lawyer.
- Saturn, Mars, and Rahu, if alone (or) together, are placed in the 6th or 12th House
- then the native becomes a criminal Lawyer.
- Ketu and Saturn built a tax lawyer.
- A strong twin Sun and Moon will ensure a successful public prosecutor. Saturn backs insurance lawyers, and Venus backs one who deals in Matrimony.
- The combinations are endless, and we have discussed the key points.

Example Chart 5

There is something known as a judicial temperament which needs to be present in an individual sitting in the judge's chair in a court of law. He is an excellent communicator who communicates with a sense of authority and with a fact-finding attitude. He communicates with his counsels and jury members with a sense of mutual respect and calmness. He needs to be a good listener and listen to the arguments of both parties with an open mind without any biases. Being in the superior position, individuals adorning the chair cannot compromise on their ethics and values. They possess a sharp intellect to see through situations and uncover the truth.

This is a horoscope of an eminent judge who had an illustrious career and was a successful civil Lawyer. Though from an agrarian family, by dint of hard work, he excelled in his law studies and made up an excellent career.

Rahu			Asc
			Jupiter
	Rasi		Moon Sun Mercury Venus
Saturn		Mars	Ketu

Excellent placement of 10th Lord Jupiter exalted in the 2nd House, which made the Judge known for his verdicts. 9th Lord in Kendra aspecting 9th House. The combination of Moon, Sun, Mercury and Venus in the 3rd House is a welcome aspect especially when Sun is extremely strong, making the judge an excellent communicator.

Rahu in the 10th is a positive arrangement, and the Rahu period was his initial years of practice and judiciary. Rahu gave him a good amount of learning, though it was a restless period for the judge. He rose to greater heights in the Dasa of Jupiter, culminating as the principal judge in a high court.

Shadbala of important planets were

Sun	173%
Mars	136%
Jupiter	128%

The planets made him versatile, logical and balanced in working. Asthakavarga of Lagna is very high at 38 points, with 9th and 10th House with 31 and 33, respectively. This made him maintain a winning streak throughout his career.

Example Chart 6

Rahu		Saturn Moon	
Asc	Rasi		Sun
			Mars Mercury Venus
	Jupiter		Ketu

This a horoscope of a successful lawyer who rose from obscurity to be a renowned person. The benefics of this chart are Sun (7th), Mars (3,10), Venus (4,9) and Saturn (1,12). All 4 planets are well placed as far as professional outlook is concerned.

Lagna Lord in Kendra with exalted 6th Lord and aspected by Jupiter from 10th is an excellent arrangement for progress and success in the chosen field. Sun in the 6th adds strength to the House and makes the natives face adverse situations. Shadbala of important planets are

Sun	115%
Jupiter	120%
Saturn	123%

which are very encouraging. Exalted 6th Lord in the 4th with the aspect of Jupiter from the 10th made the native face litigations and arguments effectively.

d) An Engineer/Scientist

Engineering is a profession which is taken up by youngsters who study science. It has generated many jobs and is a source of employment in the market. Therefore, more and more young students are willing to take up the profession. A person taking up this profession needs to be creative and possess critical thinking where they ask why and seek an answer for it. Usually, people taking up this profession need to work collaboratively. So, they need to be good team players and effective communicators. A considerable number of people undertake engineering studies these days. Very few take up higher studies in engineering or even pursue it as a profession later. Even among those who graduate, only very few join the core stream of jobs which they have preferred to study.

Astrology can illuminate who can pursue engineering and follow it up with a respectable and meaningful job. An individual taking up the profession has Mars and Saturn as their primary indicators in their planetary position.

According to career astrology, the planets responsible for the engineering profession are Mars, Mercury and Saturn. Of course, for education, Jupiter plays an important role. Mercury plays an important role in technical education and its application.

The Rasis representing the Engineering profession are Gemini, Libra, Capricorn and Aquarius. If these Rasis become 10th Bhava or House, they indicate technical education and profession. When associated with Mercury, Mars and Saturn, Rahu can encourage the subject to take up engineering. All Mercury-based stars like

Ashlesha, Jyeshtha and Revati strongly support the engineering profession.

The combination of planets in the 4th, 9th and 10th Houses for the engineering profession are:

- There is a combination of Mars and Mercury in the chart.
- There is a connection between Saturn and Mars.
- The effect of the Sun and Mercury, if an engineer pursues a government-based job, will be profound.
- Mercury and Mars indicate mechanical engineering.
- Mercury and Venus indicate information technology.
- Mercury and Mars indicate biotechnology.
- Mercury and Saturn indicate metallurgy and mines.
- Mercury and Rahu indicate nano-technology and IT.
- Mercury and Saturn can make one to get interested in civil engineering. If an engineer pursues a job, then the 6th House should be strong and the 6th Lord should be with dignity.

Example Chart 7

			Mars
Ketu	Rasi		Moon
			Rahu
Saturn Jupiter			Mercury Sun Venus Asc

This is a horoscope of a post graduate engineer from a premier institution. The person is a good student and has excelled academically from the beginning. The person has the right planetary combination to compete in different competitive exams and pursue higher studies in engineering later in life. His stars indicate excellence in his chosen field.

The native had basic education in a military school and was a board examination topper in the school final. In Mars Dasa, the native joined NDA and then graduated into the armed forces. He pursued higher education in Electronics in Rahu Dasa. In Rahu Dasa, he became a civilian and, took up a corporate job and reached the highest echelons of telecommunication companies with a good career track record.

Mercury in Lagna is exalted, and the 2nd and 9th Lord gets Neechabanga raja yoga. A conjunction of the 9th and 10th Lord is excellent for getting fame and name in a career. The combination of the 4th and 5th Lord aspecting the 10th House is a good preposition for higher studies and intelligence. Asthakavarga of the following Bhavas are excellent and, therefore augurs well for the native.

House	Points
Lagna	31
6th	28
10th	31
11th	36
9th	28

It is not a surprise if we look at the Shadbala of the key planets.

Mars	159%
Sun	153%
Moon	127%
Mercury	120%
Jupiter	117%

Overall, it is an excellent horoscope in terms of intelligence, hard work and integrity.

Example Chart 8

			Rahu Saturn
Ketu	Rasi		
Moon Mars	Venus Jupiter	Sun Mercury Asc	

A person who pursues science as a subject has a quest for knowledge. Saturn and Mercury are the planets which help them in their pursuit of knowledge and help them in reaching their destination. Ketu is the planet that waters the seed inside the researcher to find new things in their area of expertise.

This is the horoscope of a Nobel Laureate in Physics. He achieved this great feat when infrastructure and support were minimal for scientific research. Look at the academic brilliance. Sun and Mercury forming Budha Aditya Yoga in the Lagna itself.

First-rate benefic Saturn in 10th House aspecting 4th along with Rahu made him pursue serious research as his vocation. Moon Dasa enabled his fertile imagination and studies. The influence of Rahu made him pursue exploratory research in its Dasa.

Houses like Lagna, 6th,10th and 11th are rendered strong by more than 29 Bindus in Asthakavarga. Jupiter and Venus in 2nd place enabled the native to communicate effortlessly through research and various exploratory studies.

e) Self-employed

A self-employed person has an exploratory mind. They have keen observation skills by which they understand the functioning of a trade and the basic work parameters. They find their niche area of expertise and fit themselves into the system they operate in. They are self-motivated to stand up against all odds and disciplined people internally driven by passion.

It is this budding passion inside people which becomes the foundation for a successful business. For a self-employed the 2nd, the 6th and 10th house are of great importance. The 2nd house shows the kind of wealth the person would accumulate. The 6th house gives an idea about the person's work environment and the 10th house shows the individual's career choice. We will look at certain points of Astrological interest for self-employed people. Here are the astrological factors which enable a self-employed person:

- Lagnathipathi in 10th place
- 10th Lord in Lagna
- Exchange between 1st and 10th Lord
- Kendra Lords strongly placed in 10th House with dignity
- Exalted 4th House Lord
- 10th House aspected by benefic planets with dignity

- The 6th, 8th and 12th Lord should not be associated with Lagna or the 10th House. Otherwise, it will be a deterrent combination for self-employment
- If the 10th House, 10th Lord and Lagna Lord are with dignity and strong, Then, the business will have growth prospects.

If the 10th Lord is weak and debilitated, then the native will not have an interest in self-employment.

2. Combinations for various career options

Job	Signs
Government	Sun and Mars in 10th
Medicine	10th House, Sun, Mars, Saturn and Rahu
Engineering	Mercury, Mars and Saturn in the 10th
Judiciary	Jupiter and Mercury in the 10th
Bank	10th House. Mercury, Jupiter and Saturn
Real Estate	Mars in 10th (or) 4th
Educational Institutions	2nd, 4th and 10th place Mercury and Jupiter
Government	10th House Moon and Venus
Hotels	10th and 4th place Venus
Politics	10th House, Sun, Mars and Moon
Motor	10th and 4th House Venus

We can list many more combinations, but this would do for now. By experience, it would be possible to zero in on the exact profession.

The astrological position helps an individual know the kind of profession they can profess according to the position and the suitability of the stars and their personality traits. It is good to take a deeper understanding of people's astrological position and then choose a path for themselves in which people can make decent choices and engrave a path to success and happiness with the help of a little guidance. People can read this chapter and get their astrological position checked by an astrologer for better understanding.

CHAPTER 4

PLANETARY COMBINATION FOR POLITICS

*S*ince time unknown, stars have predicted the future and the life of individuals, countries, and states. Ever since the Vedic era, astrological positions were used to predict the political situations that would prevail in a country. An astrologer could predict and forewarn the rulers regarding the different crises and adversity a nation would face in future. The astronomers used their knowledge to predict the position of stars and planets to make mathematical models and help astrologers make predictions for the future. Therefore, from the Vedic times, astrology has been used for all significant events.

The World of Astrological Politics and Politicians

- The days of the monarchs are over, and most countries elect their governing bodies to power. People taking up this career

are usually stable-headed and extroverts by personality to lead a nation or state. Normally, politicians prefer politics as a career for the following purposes:
- Doing service to people
- To make a difference
- Power and money
- Name and fame
- To give back to the community

The belief in astrology and the effect of the placement of stars has grown many folds over the years. People look for good astrologers for predictions about their future life is a fact that cannot be ruled out. We find most astrologers making predictions about political movements in the country before an election period, depicting the changes which the country would face with the change in leadership.

A politician is someone elected to govern the nation. Since politicians occupy an important position in the Government and society, their birth chart combination of stars and planets would be different and extremely special. It would be interesting to see the special features that make one a successful politician.

In classical astrological works like BPHS (or) Phaladeepika several combinations are given for successful political careers. In the olden days, they were called Raja Yogas. Today, these Yogas manifest in different ways. Usually, it is seen that the four planets

Sun, Saturn, Mars and Jupiter play a crucial role in the life of a successful politician.

Planets which play a crucial role

- A well-placed Saturn in an individual's birth chart indicates a ruler, politician or the head of a state. Saturn is the planet of masses. The placement of Saturn in 3rd, 6th, 11th and 10th makes one a people-based politician.
- The Sun is the royal planet, indicating the rule of power. It gives one the will to rule and enables one to get government support.
- A well-placed moon in the life of a politician means the person has great mental strength, which is needed for ruling the masses. The moon is also a royal planet. It reflects an individual's emotional balance and mental agility and makes one travel a lot with good intuition, which is essential for a politician.
- Jupiter is the planet of expansion for the individual and the society alike. It stands for righteousness, and the individual would succeed as a politician. It gives an individual integrity to be in public life. The association of Jupiter and the moon will give tenacity for an individual to govern.
- Rahu brings diplomacy, deception and tact, which are essential for a politician. It makes the individual influential and gives them a personality which impresses the masses. Rahu in 3rd, 6th and 10th ensures success in politics.

Houses and Politics

- Important Houses for politics are 1,2,3,6,7,9 and 10:
- 1st House represents the soul and personality of an individual, and therefore, it becomes important.

- 2nd House represents speech and communication skills, which are essential for a politician.
- The 3rd House stands for courage, the ability to generate fame and travel frequently.
- The 5th House reflects the intelligence, creativity and cleverness of the politician.
- The 6th House indicates one's power to resist adversity and emerge victorious. It also represents the ability to thrive in competition.
- 9th House signifies the thinking process, ability to make choices and fortune.
- 10th House represents the career or profession of an individual. It also reflects hard work, integrity and a moral code of conduct.

Yogas for success

Raja Yogas plays a vital role in creating a politician. Some of them are:

Dhana Yoga: The Dhana Yoga signifies the wealth a person would accumulate in their lifetime. It is the relationship between 2nd, 5th, 9th and 11th Houses.

Gajakesari Yoga: A person under the influence of this yoga has sharp intellectual capability and leads a prosperous life. Moon and Jupiter are in Kendra to each other. It gives mental and physical strength and the tenacity to thrive in competition.

Karmajiva Yoga: This yoga, as the name suggests, is the house of the karma of the Individual, which suggests their purpose of work. Strong Mercury occupies the 10th house with dignity. The native will have a name and fame in his lifetime.

Chandra Mangala Yoga: An individual under the influence of this yoga gets name, fame and financial success in life. Moon and Mars either conjunct (or) aspecting each other. Such people will exhibit manipulating qualities and thrive even in difficult situations.

Pancha Maha Purusha Yoga: With the help of this yoga, a person gets name, fame, respect in society, prosperity and glory as well. Mars, Mercury, Jupiter, Venus and Saturn are placed in their own (or) exaltation in Kendras.

Vargottama Yoga: This yoga shows an individual's inner valour and physical strength. If more than 3 planets are in Vargottama, the native will be valorous and conquer his enemies.

Neecha Bhanga Yoga: We have discussed this elsewhere in the book.

Dharma Karmadhipathy Yoga: The people under the influence of this yoga are usually high-ranking officials in the government machinery. The association between the 9th and 10th Lord with benefic placement.

Important combinations

1. Sun with dignity is placed in the 9th or 10th house
2. Sun and Mercury conjunction in the 2nd, 6th and 12th Houses aspected by Jupiter
3. Jupiter in Kendra and association of 9th, 10th and 7^{th}House
4. Rahu must be connected to the 10th House and well-placed If Mars and Saturn with dignity are associated with the 4th and 10^{th}House

5. If the Sun and Moon are in their exalted or own sign. If they are placed in Kendra and Kona, they will deliver the desired results.
6. Lagna Lord occupies the 9th House in Navamsa and also Vargottama
7. Combination of 1st, 2nd, 4th, 5th, 9th, 10th and 11th in any form with dignity

Example Chart 1

Jupiter Venus	Ketu		
Sun Mercury Asc	Rasi		
Moon			
	Saturn	Rahu Mars	

This is a chart of the former president of the United States of America. He had a distinct role in restructuring the American society to a large extent. Aquarius rises with Mercury and the Sun in Lagna, making him intelligent and one with a balanced mind.

Lagna Lord Saturn aspected by Jupiter and in Kendra was very strong. Yogakaraka Venus exalted in the 2nd with Jupiter, the planet of expansion, indicating excellent integrity, character and conduct.

The excellent placement of Venus speaks about the good support of his mother. He was an intellectual and experienced growth of his character in all capacities when he was self-educating himself. Before taking a political career, he served society selflessly. He was deeply inspired by literature and was a philanthropist at heart. A self-made man, he stood for his thoughts and beliefs all his life. Two malefic Rahu and Mars afflict the 9th House. Therefore, his father was not of much support. You can look at the position of the moon in the 12th aspected by Saturn. He would have been, at times, subjected to emotional disturbances. Strong Lagna, 2nd, 4th, 5th, 7th and 10th Houses elevated him to the position of president.

In the classical text Jataka Tatwa, when Saturn, Sun and Mars are in the Kendras or the 10th, 7th and $4^{th,}$ respectively, death will happen due to assassination. In this case, Saturn is in the 10th, 7th aspected by Sun and 4th aspected by Mars. Hence, the fatal end. Being born in a log cabin and rising to be the president is not an easy task. It was a long and unbelievable journey, and the strength of his horoscope is an indication of his achievements.

Example Chart 2

			Rahu
			Moon Asc
	Rasi		
			Saturn
Jupiter Ketu	Sun	Mercury Venus	Mars

This is a horoscope of an Indian Prime Minister. Lagna Lord is in its own House and, therefore, very strong. The individual's early life was uneventful as he was born into a rich family with a silver spoon in his mouth. The individual received higher education in prestigious colleges in India and abroad. As an educated youth, he believed in democracy and secularism. He was extremely well-read, overcame his negative thoughts and beliefs and contributed to the growth of the country at large. The Lagna is hemmed between two malefic.

As we observe the chart, we find the native had a noble countenance because of the presence of the Moon in Lagna. Sun in Scorpio can bring forth little contradictory ideas, but the native overcame this because of the strong Moon in Lagna. Jupiter aspecting the 2nd House makes him humane and, therefore, enjoys the support of the masses. His intellectual achievements were mainly because of the presence of Mercury in the 2nd House of Navamsa.

Jupiter's ruling in the 6th House made him resilient and one with strong socioeconomic ideas. Venus's placement in his House in the 4th ensured his health and comfort. The horoscope suffers from Kalasarpa Yoga and, therefore, extreme sensitivity. Overall, the Lagna 3rd, 4th, 5th, 6th and 9th are well fortified. 10th Lord Mars aspects its House, which is an excellent arrangement.

Example Chart 3

	Saturn Jupiter	Ketu	Moon Mars
Mercury	Rasi		
Sun Venus			Asc
	Rahu		

This is a horoscope of a former president of the United States of America. Lagna is aspected by both benefics Jupiter and Mercury, which strengthens it. 1st and 10th Lord strong in the 6th enables the native to face stiff competition and succeed. Chandra Mangala Yoga is in the 11th House with Mars as Yogakaraka. From Chandra Lagna, Raja Yoga is formed because of the conjunction of the 9th and 10th Lord. This took the native to the presidency.

Chandra Mangala Yoga happens in the house of Mercury, and Lagna is powerfully aspected. This made him bring about notable changes in legislation. 6th House is afflicted in a way and, therefore, has a physical disability. These planetary combinations made the native reach the highest position in the country.

Example chart: 4

		Moon	Venus
Ketu	Rasi		Mercury Sun
Saturn Jupiter			Mars Rahu
		Asc	

This is a horoscope of a former President of the USA.

Sun is placed in the 10th with Mercury, forming Budha-Aditya Nipuna Yoga. This means a conjunction of the 9th and 11th Lord is happening in the 10th, which is a Raja Yoga. Saturn, the Karaka for masses, is in the 4th aspecting the 10th, generating people's support. Lagna was rendered strong by Venus, which energized his personality and soul. The Sun and Saturn played a clear role in elevating him to the post of president.

Example Chart 5

Rahu		Asc	
Saturn Mars	Rasi		
	Moon	Mercury Jupiter Sun Venus	Ketu

This is the chart of a man who played a significant role in gaining the country's independence and restructuring the now independent states of India. He was a learned man who believed in the democratic set-up of the country and its secular state. He was a man of very strong integrity who believed in contributing even in the most challenging times. The Lagna Lord is in his own House, not aspected by any malefic, and was, therefore, strong. 10th Lord in his House with exalted Mars made him the Iron Man of India. He played an extraordinary role in shaping the country during Independence. The 6th House was made strong by the presence of 4 planets, which allowed him to fight adversity and bring in the union of India. Moon gets Neechabanga and, therefore, a stern communicator. Ketu in the 5th may make him appear to be dogmatic sometimes. Again, Saturn, the Sun and the 10th House took the native to great heights and brought him to the political limelight.

For a person to be a good politician who shines and glows in the eyes of the masses, the astrological position is extremely special. Sun, a very strong planet, is in an exalted position and ensures leadership and a powerful position for the individual. The moon in the chart strengthens the mind to make decisions, and Jupiter's position helps create goodwill among the masses. A strong position of Jupiter shows the person would work for justice and the larger causes of society, bringing in name and fame for the person. The position of Mars empowers the fighting spirit and helps them to stand against adversity. The 9th, 10th and 12th houses should be running Dasas of functional benefit to other Lagnas. As we proceed, we will have a greater understanding of the different positions of the stars in different houses and their effect on human life.

CHAPTER 5

CAREER IN THE FILM INDUSTRY & SPORTING ARENA

*T*he world of cinema and sport is unique in creativity, skill set and glamour. We all are a part of the society attracted to this shimmering world of light, charm and enchantment. These two areas of interest have a charm amongst the younger generation. They can unite people across the globe with an interest in similar passions.

People might stand divided due to political and economic reasons across borders. Still, they come together to attend sporting events and cultural initiatives and appreciate cinematic excellence at various award functions.

The entertainment world is very attractive to people worldwide due to the name, fame and money that comes with it. Many youngsters make huge sacrifices by putting up a humongous amount of trouble to get selected for a movie or any motion picture initiative taken up by a producer or director.

Similarly, in the world of sports, the contestant has to go through various levels of selection procedure. The athlete needs to play at the state and national level and then get selected for international sporting events to finally get acclaimed for international accolades and earn fame for themselves and their country. The journey is long, and the effort is colossal.

The world of cinema and sports attracts innumerable people across the globe due to the glamour factor attached to it. Many young people aspire to enter the industry to register their name on the wall of fame. The effort of all usually does not get paid *off* due to many reasons. Not all reach great heights. There should be enough talent, temperament, endurance and professional acumen. Only a few reach the top. The reasons for the success can be well understood through the spectrum of Astrology.

While many might give the credit to the artistic acumen, showmanship and skills of individuals, there are also the stars who have a fate pre-decided and are writing a story of which we are unaware. Many spirited, zealous and dynamic people are left behind without a significant story to share, and ordinary people make it to the top because they were born with the stars at the right places. Combined with their hard work and the spirit of fighting an uphill battle, they spiral high into fame and name. The planetary combination, the strength of various houses, the timing of events and the Yogas give a clear indication as to the success of the native. It is said that people with great acting skills and who make it to the top of the ladder have Venus and Mercury in a strong position in their birth chart.

Important Houses

As per Vedic Astrology, the 3rd, 5th and 10th House signify performance in the cine field. The responsible planets are Venus, Moon and Mercury. Jupiter stands for fortune, and the Sun gives rise to fame. A strong connection between 3rd, 5th, 6th, 10th and 11th promises enduring success is established.

Planets

Moon

To become a superstar, the moon's position in an individual's birth chart plays a significant role. The moon signifies the vital attributes of acting and singing (vocals). It reflects and enables an individual to express one's emotions appropriately. If the moon, Mars and Venus are involved, the person will be part of action-oriented movies. If the moon and Saturn are combined, the actor will be part of a movie with social messages. People under the strong influence of the moon are charismatic and can go ahead and win the hearts of millions of people.

Mars

Natives under the influence of Mars signify energy and action. All action stars, technicians and supporting actors are under the influence of Mars. People, usually under the influence of this planet, have the strength to take the troughs and the peaks coming in the way of their careers.

Jupiter

The effect of the planet Jupiter is huge. Usually, actors who go ahead and sign up for huge-budget movies and blockbuster hits are under the strong influence of this planet. People under its influence show great artistic talent, and they have luck by their side when they are pursuing their careers. With the power of Jupiter, one can become a director. Of course, movies have different genres, all of which happen by combining various planets with Jupiter.

Venus

The strong presence of Venus in the life of an individual creates a drive to pursue acting as a career. People under the influence are truly driven by philosophy and are full of creative attitudes and instincts. People with a strong influence of Venus can be actors, stylists, makeup artists, vocalists, music directors and choreographers.

The planet combination and the role which it leads to are:

Venus, Mercury, Jupiter, Moon	Director
Venus, Mercury, Moon	Dancer, Choreographer
Mercury, Venus, Moon, Jupiter	Music composer
Mars, Mercury, Saturn	Technician
Mercury, Jupiter, Venus	Producer, Distributor
Mercury, Venus	Publicity, Communication

One must keep in mind the Raj Yogas and Dasa/Gochara will determine the success level.

Example Chart 1

Rahu		
Jupiter	Rasi	
Mars Moon		Asc
Venus Mercury	Sun	Ketu Saturn

This is a horoscope of a leading actor. The actor under discussion was the son of an ordinary man, and his life started in complete anonymity. During his school education, he showed great interest towards the theatre and performed many shows during his school years. At a very tender age, his skill won the hearts of many people who watched him perform. As time passed, he took up many jobs for a living. He worked as a carpenter, a coolie and then finally got recruited as a conductor by the state transport department.

- 3rd and 10th Lord in conjunction with Mercury in the 5th aspecting the 11th. Lord of Lagna in the 7th House aspecting the lagna very strongly.
- 5th Lord is aspecting the Lagna sitting with dignity in the 6th.

- Yogakaraka Mars exalted with the Moon in the 6th Moon aspecting his own House the 12th.
- Benefic planets on both sides of the Moon (1-2)

The above planetary combinations gave the actor great success and a tremendous fan following. His action performance is considered to be unique.

Chart 2

Asc Moon			Ketu
	Rasi		Jupiter
Mars			
Rahu	Venus	Mercury Saturn Sun	

The actor under discussion is a person who does not belong to a family of actors and actresses. He came from a standard middle-class family and pursued his love for the art of acting right from his childhood. His life rose from anonymity to the limelight at a very early age. He won the President's award as a child artist and rose to shine as a star at a very tender age. While his other brothers and sisters pursued higher education, he remained with his love for acting.

- Venus in the 9th aspected by exalted Jupiter is an excellent placement. Lagna Lord exalted in the 5th aspected by Yogakaraka Mars.
- Yogakaraka Mars exalted and aspected by Jupiter and placed in the 11th House
- The exchange of Houses between the Lagna Lord and the 5th (Jupiter, Moon) is a Raja Yoga.
- 10th House has Rahu aspected by an exalted Saturn.
- 11th and 12th Lord associated with 6th and 5th Lord.

Considered to be a genius in acting. The versatile actor also has a big fan following. He has won many awards and acted in multilingual films.

Example Chart 3

Rahu Venus			
Mars Sun	Rasi		Jupiter
Mercury Saturn			
	Moon		Ketu Asc

This is a horoscope of a Hollywood actress. The actress earned fame and a huge fan following. She was the highest paid in her time and had performed for nearly 3 decades. From the tinsel town rose a teeny-weeny girl to be a star of her times. A girl born with a silver spoon in her mouth had dual citizenship in Britain and the USA. Her father, who was an American art dealer and her mother, a well-known actress, brought up their children in the luxurious environment of Beverly Hills.

- Venus, a first-rate Yogakaraka exalted in the 7th House, is aspected by exalted Jupiter.
- 4th and 7th Lord Jupiter exalted in the 11th and aspected by 5th Lord
- Saturn forming sasa yoga
- Rahu, in conjunction with Venus, is a strong placement.
- 8th and 12th Lord in the 6th are giving Vipareetha Raja Yoga.

Chart 4

	Asc Venus Mercury Sun Ketu	Mars	
Moon	Rasi		Jupiter Saturn
		Rahu	

This chart depicts the life of a famous film director, screenplaywright, author, music composer and lyricist of his time. He came from a family which had a literary inclination. Father, a poet and mother, a homemaker, brought up their son in the most traditional way. As a child, the director went to a government school in West Bengal and later attended one of the best colleges in Kolkata. He was sent to Shantiniketan, the boiling pot of art and literature in Eastern India, to pursue his interest in art and literature.

After passing out, the director joined an advertising company where he was known for his artistic excellence. Soon, he came across the writer of some imminent books, which inspired him to put it across as a motion picture. However, he did not have the money to make the movie, and he had to pool his own resources for the making of the movie.. Let us analyse his birth chart in detail.

- Lagna has Budha Aditya Yoga.
- The conjunction of 9th and 10th Lord in the 5th brings in Dharma Karma Yoga.
- Exchange of Lord of Houses - 1st & 2nd are very strong
- Venus and Mercury in Lagna are aspected by Jupiter.
- 9th Lord Guru since it is Vargottama will become a first-rate benefic to the native.

Chart 5

Mercury	Sun Venus	Saturn	Ketu
	Rasi		
Mars Jupiter			Asc
Rahu Moon			

This is a chart of the world's best cricketer. Son of a novelist and a poet, he took up a love for cricket at the age of eleven. He was good for his age, and under the guardianship of his elder brother, he was put to practice under one of the best coaches of his time. He showed extraordinary skills, due to which he was brought as a forerunner and at the tender age of sixteen, he became a part of the Indian cricket team. As a child prodigy, he brought many accolades to the country and played great cricket, so he was considered the God of Cricket.

The horoscope clearly shows the native's personality, sporting acumen, career, health and wealth.

- Mars elevated in the 6th House, being a Yogakaraka gives courage, determination and lots of physical energy.
- Venus in the 9th bestows fortune.

- Sun in the 9th house makes him hard-working and dutiful. Sun is exalted, which assures success in his career. Not only was he consistent for nearly 2 decades, but he also earned a lot of wealth.
- The Dasa of Rahu gave him the much-needed shot in the arm.

Example chart 6

	Saturn		
Rahu Mars	Rasi		
		Ketu	
Mercury Moon	Venus Sun	Jupiter Asc	

This is the horoscope of an international chess player. He has been known for his acumen nationally and internationally across the globe. His father was a high-ranking railway official, and his mother was an influential socialite and a chess enthusiast. The youngest of the three siblings, the player learnt his first lessons in chess at the age of six from his mother. While his knowledge of chess was good, he learnt the complexity of the game at Manila, where his father was posted.

After his early learning stages, he kept himself trained and performed excellently at the sub-junior chess championship, where he won the award. At the young age of 15, he won the Asian

Junior Championship. At the age of 18, he became the first Indian grandmaster and went ahead to defeat the Russian grandmaster. His skill was appreciated, and at 18, he was awarded the Padma Shri. He has won accolades nationally and internationally. He is a legendary character and is looked up by all players worldwide. Let us analyse his birth chart in detail.

- Lagna Lord is in the 2nd House with the 11th Lord (Sun, Venus).
- Jupiter is in Lagna, and therefore, Lagna becomes stronger.
- 9th and 10th Lord conjoined and aspecting the 9th House
- (Moon, Mercury) Yogakaraka Saturn gets Neechabanga being in Kendra and becomes stronger by the aspect of Jupiter.
- Rahu/Mars makes him intelligent.
- For sports, the Mars and Mercury combination makes the difference. Their association with 1st, 3rd, 6th and 10th Houses makes the difference. The more Raj Yogas found in the horoscope, the greater the success.

Most of the sporting personalities have Mars-dominated horoscopes. The temperament of these personalities is one of energy, confidence and self-belief. They are usually self-driven people who derive energy from their achievements and failures. Real talent usually finds energy from their accomplishments and the accolades they win over a lifetime.

CHAPTER 6

CAREER AND FOREIGN SETTLEMENT

*A*n exploratory bird inside us wants to see the world and explore the terrain, culture, customs and activities of other countries and places. Many travelers are moving around with an itinerary list in their hands.

There is yet another set of people who want to go ahead and settle abroad for the sake of their studies, career and future life. The belief and practice are catching up fast with people in our country. People strongly believe that studying abroad gives them an added advantage and edge over people pursuing a career in India. It is believed that people working abroad get more exposure and they are a more employable resource. This is, by and large, true in many respects. People working and studying abroad are more compatible with the new environment, more flexible with their communication skills and more confident. They are aware of the needs and demands of the institutions and the employers abroad.

Many well-educated states in India have at least one member of their family working or studying abroad. Some of the major states which lead the list are all the states from Southern India, Punjab, Gujarat, Maharashtra, etc. There is a huge attraction for people from the IT sector, young doctors and ambitious business people who want to go abroad and try their luck by doing a job or investing in some business. People are greatly attracted to countries like the USA, Europe, especially the UK, Canada, Australia, New Zealand and many Asian countries like Malaysia, Hong Kong and Singapore.

Many students aspire to study and settle abroad because of the prospects of a better job and standard of living. All the universities in the United States are flooded with Indian students, especially in the tech field. Going abroad can easily be predicted through systemic Astrological studies. Since foreign settlement is a topic of interest for many youngsters in India, Astrological opinions can be a shot in the arm. Marriage can be one of the prospects for settling abroad. The indications are pronounced in astrological charts.

According to the latest data shared by the Indian government, nearly 8 lakh people travel abroad to study for higher education. People travel to Europe, the USA, Canada, New Zealand and Australia. However, not all find themselves in their chosen destination for their studies and jobs.

The planet Saturn plays a major role in studies and jobs abroad. There are many houses which influence the life of an individual for foreign settlement.

The signs are of three types:

- Chara Rasi (or) movable signs: Aries, Cancer, Libra and Capricorn
- Sthira Rasi (or) fixed sign: Taurus, Leo, Scorpio, Aquarius
- Common sign (or) dual sign: Gemini, Virgo, Sagittarius, Pisces

People dominated by the Chara Rashi are people who wanderlust or are basically in love with travelling. They have something special by which they tend to adjust and stay in newer circumstances and easily escape difficult situations. It is the rasi of industrious people with the mindset of an achiever.

People under the influence of the Sthira rasi are like the stones in the sea. They are usually not the kind of people who prefer to settle abroad. They are averse to changing their jobs frequently and love sticking to their old employment. Such people block their chances of studying and working abroad.

Sthira Rasi (or) fixed signs do not support settlement abroad. Planets in these Rasis make a person stay put in one place. Naturally, when people have more planets in Sthira (or) fixed Rasi, they do not show a change in their preferences. Common signs act both ways, and they love to make short travels.

People born in common signs may settle in a foreign land if other strong astrological reasons are found. Out of these three types, the one which encourages foreign travel is Chara Rasi.

Therefore, one having these four Rasis as 1,3,9,10, or 12 Houses may settle abroad or frequently travel. When planets are placed in the above Rasis, the natives frequently change nature and, therefore, tend to travel.

Watery signs, namely Cancer, Scorpio and Pisces, are very important for foreign travel and settlement. Planets falling in fiery, earthy and airy signs do not enable foreign settlement.

Significant planets

The planets significant for foreign travel are the Rahu/Ketu axis, Moon, Saturn and Venus. If the dignity and dasa of the above four planets are excellent, then chances of foreign travel and settlement are higher.

Rahu is an essential factor in foreign travel, especially if they are in 3rd, 4th, 9th, 10th and 12th Houses. When connected to the 9th or the 12th House, Rahu brings in yoga for studies abroad.

Rahu Dasa makes a native to travel. If Rahu is conjoint with the 7th, 8th, 9th or 12th Lord, there is a likelihood of foreign travel.

When the moon is in a strong position, it denotes a change in place, bringing the yoga to travel to different places. The moon's role is also crucial since it is the 4th Lord of the Kalapurusha Chart. If the moon is placed in a Kendra, namely 1,4,7 or 10th House, then the native is widely travelled. Lagna or ascendant assumes a lot of importance. If the Lagna Lord is placed in the 12th or the 12th Lord in Lagna, the native settles abroad.

The 4th House stands for home country, and if it is in a strong position, it indicates foreign travel and settlement. If there is a conjunction or strong aspect between the Lagna Lord, 9th Lord and 12th Lord and if the relationship happens in a movable sign, then there are strong indications for foreign travel. It is also a sign of relationships and family. It also shows the person is concerned and will spend much time on his family duty.

The third House indicates frequent short travels, and the 12th long distance travels. The moon and Venus in the 12th house show foreign settlement and travel, and if these planets are either conjoined (or) associated in some way, then there is a likelihood of settling abroad.

If Jupiter aspects any of the combinations (or) arrangements we have discussed in the above paragraphs, then the trip will be a success.

Houses and impact

- 1st House signifies the soul and personality of the native. It also shows the general temperament of the person. Foreign settlement is likely if this House is associated with the 3rd, 7th and 12th Lord.
- 3rd House indicates travel and, therefore, a foreign settlement. It also shows the inclinations, interests and hobbies of the native.
- 4th House indicates homeland. If this is afflicted, then one might have to live far away. It also indicates a person's relationship with a maternal figure in their life and their belief in domestic life.
- 7th House indicates partnership in business, romantic liaisons, relationship with spouse, partnership in business and foreign travel. If the 7th House is strong and connected with the 3rd or 12th House, there are indications of foreign travel.

- The 9th House is the house of journeys and thinking processes. It is a house which is willing to accept change and expand the universe according to the changing environment and temperament.
- If the 9th Lord is with dignity and the 9th House unafflicted, then one enjoys a good life abroad. If the 10th is connected with the 3rd and 12th Lords, then there is a tendency to settle abroad.
- If malefic planets like the Sun, Saturn, Mars and Rahu occupy the 12th House, one may not enjoy their foreign stay.

Foreign settlement after marriage

Marriage can make an individual settle abroad if the astrological positions are right. Many men and women have the dream of settling abroad after their marriage. However, only if the right yoga exists is it possible. Usually, if Mercury is placed in the 12th house and Shani in the 7th house, the yoga of settling abroad after marriage becomes possible. Let us now examine under what Astrological arrangements one is forced to settle abroad after marriage.

- 7th House connection with 8th, 9th and 12th Houses makes one travel abroad after marriage.
- When the 12th Lord is in its own House
- Exchange between 9th and 12th Lords
- Lord of the 7th House in the 11th House
- Saturn in the 7th House with a strong 3rd Lord

Foreign travel and settlement are energised by the Dasa of the 9th Lord, 12th Lord or Rahu. The planets in the 9th and 12th can also activate a foreign settlement.

Example Chart 1

		Venus Saturn	Moon Sun Mercury
	Rasi		Asc Ketu
Mars Rahu			
	Jupiter		

This is the birth chart of a person who spent his childhood in Germany and is currently settled in Australia and doing well. If you observe the birth chart, the Lagna Lord in the 12th with strong 3rd and 12th Lord Mercury indicates foreign settlement. The presence of the 2nd Lord in the 12th House adds to the reason. Rahu in the 7th, that too in movable sign with exalted Yogakaraka, is another compelling reason for a successful foreign settlement.

The 9th House Lord in the watery sign is another strong reason for studies and settlement abroad. Exalted Mars is very good for a career, status and money in a foreign land. The 4th and 7th Lord connection placed in the 11th indicates travel. Whenever the 7th Lord comes in contact with the 4th House, the native settles in a foreign land. Venus strong in Rohini Nakshatra ensures name, fame and success.

Vipareeth Raja Yoga involving the 6th and 12th Lord ensures foreign travel.

Example Chart 2

	Mars	Venus	Sun Mercury Jupiter
		Rasi	Ketu
Rahu			
Moon Saturn	Asc		

In the birth chart displayed above, the Lagna Lord in the 6th in its own House is aspecting the 12th House, which is a strong indicator for foreign settlement. The 7th and 12th Lord Venus in its own House aspecting the Lagna is a compelling reason for the travel of the native. The marriage of the native was by choice because of the strong influence of Venus. After studying abroad during Sun Dasa, the native returned to India, settled in the UK in the Moon Dasa, and is doing well. The presence of Sun, Mercury and Jupiter in the 8th lends credence to the native's decision.

Example Chart 3

		Rahu	Jupiter
Saturn	Rasi		Asc
	Mars Ketu Moon	Venus	Sun Mercury

In the above birth chart, the Lagna Lord gets Neechabanga; therefore, it is in 5th place with a strong Yogakaraka. Mars is a Yogakaraka planet of 5th and 10th, which brings prosperity, name and fame to the natives and, therefore, success in a foreign land. 3rd and 12th Lord exalted in the 3rd House with the Sun forming Budha Aditya Nipuna Yoga. The natives first migrated to the Gulf and have now settled in Canada since 1996. The migration took place in the Dasa of Mercury.

Example Chart 4

	Moon	Asc Ketu	
Saturn	Rasi		
Venus Sun Mercury Mars			
	Rahu	Jupiter	

In the above birth chart, the Lagna Lord is well placed in the 9th friendly House.

Yogakaraka Saturn in 10th in its own House. The 3rd Lord in the 12th movable Rasi in the chart is strong, which is a strong indicator. The native is running Moon Dasa right now. The native migrated from India to the US. Since the 12th House is made strong by the aspect of Jupiter and Gaja Kesari Yoga. Four planets, Venus, Sun, Mars and Mercury are in movable sign (or) Chara Rasi. Exalted Rahu in the 7th is a compelling reason.

In all the four charts, there are strong indications of settling abroad, a successful career and a prosperous life.

Life in any part of the world or settlement after marriage is pre-decided according to the time of birth, which can be decoded with the help of the birth chart.

These days, many young people want to know about their prospects of settling abroad with a job or their marriage process. Make yourself doubly sure that your *efforts* are moving towards the right destination by taking the right astrological help at the right time.

CHAPTER 7

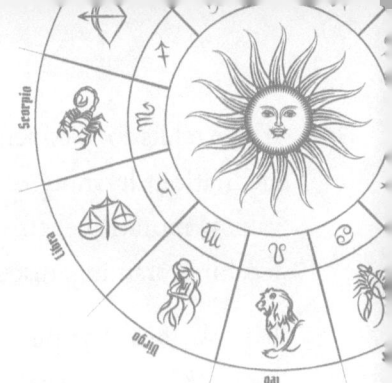

FOUNDATION- EDUCATION

*N*eedless to say, education remains the solid foundation for one's career. Education leads to the formation of appropriate skill sets, enabling a person to pursue a proper career. We have seen instances where one's education cannot directly correlate with his career. In other words, he may pursue some other business or profession unrelated to his educational background. This was more so in the past few decades, and the situation is changing slowly during the current decade. Education will play a profound role in a person's career and must be understood from the right perspective. We will now see what factors influence a person's education, leading to a successful career and lifelong achievements. One needs to interpret career benefits for a native to ensure what kind of education is in store for the native. You can now read about the various factors of Astrology which would contribute to the education of the person, leading to successful employment or career.

If one refers to Wikipedia, education is defined as "the process of facilitation, learning or the acquisition of knowledge, skills and values, morals, beliefs and habits." Education methods include teaching, training, discussions and directed research.

It is obvious that purposeful education is essential for all of us across the various age groups. Education is a continuous process. Now, let us see what planets or Houses would be responsible for getting the best education during a lifetime.

Education and Houses from Lagna

The following Houses from Lagna stand for different levels of education that one pursues.

2nd Primary education
4th Up to graduation
5th Post graduation
9th Research and exploration

These Houses play an essential role in giving opportunities for individuals to study. Considering certain circumstances, it is common to note that even an intelligent person may not get an opportunity to study higher education. Necessarily, these Houses are strengthened enough for the desired education levels.

Significator of Education

The Karaka for education is Mercury. It should be well placed in its own House, exaltation, Moolatrikona or in a friend's house.

It should not be associated with (or) aspected by a malefic. Mercury should be placed in a Kendra or Trikona from Lagna. As an exception, it can be placed in 8th when combined with the Sun. The conjunction (or) combination of Sun and Mercury goes by the name Budha Aditya Yoga, which results in the native enjoying excellent levels of intelligence and application of mind. If the well-placed Mercury is in conjunction with the benefic and natural friend, then it might enhance the quality of education. If well-placed Mercury is aspected by benefic, there are several advantages.

House Analysis

2nd House: The second House indicates primary education. If the 2nd Lord is debilitated, in inimical signs and Dusthanas, there will be a break in primary education. The 2nd House should not be afflicted.

4th House: The 4th Lord in Lagna will give happiness and a good education. If the 4th Lord is placed in Kendra/Konas identical with his own house or exaltation, then excellent education prospects for the native. If placed in 6th, 8th, or 12th, then there will be disappointing results for the natives regarding education.

5th House: Signifies intelligence and memory power. The 4th and 5th Lord together controls the grasping power of the individual. If both Lords are well placed or associated, then there will be good prospects for the native on the strength of this House, whether the individual will do higher studies or not. 5th House also indicates the diagnostic and analytical power of the individual.

9th House: The strength of the 9th Lord and 9th House denotes the individual's exploratory power. Due research is possible by the 9th Lord and the strength of the 9th House.

Planets responsible for higher education are Mercury and Jupiter. Even if one of them is associated with the 9th House or 9th Lord, the native becomes a research scholar.

Example 1

	Rasi		Rahu Saturn
Ketu			
Mars	Venus Jupiter Moon	Sun Mercury Asc	

This is a horoscope of a research scholar. Lagna has Budha-Aditya Yoga, meaning the native is an intelligent person. 9th Lord in Lagna Kendra made him do exploratory studies. 4th Lord is in the 10th aspecting 4th House. 11th Lord is getting Neechabhanga because of the placement of 4th Lord. Excellent horoscope for pursuing higher education.

Example 2

Lagna has exalted Jupiter, who is the 9th Lord. Mercury was exalted in the 3rd House. The 4th House Lord is in his own house with Yogakaraka Mars. The 5th has the moon, which attains Neechabanga because of the placement of Mars in the 4th. He was an outstanding scholar with a meritorious academic and technocratic stint with the government.

Rahu			
	Rasi		Asc Jupiter
Saturn	Moon	Venus Mars	Mercury Sun Ketu

Example 3:

			Ketu
	Rasi		
Moon			Jupiter Saturn Mars
Asc Rahu		Venus	Mercury Sun

This is the horoscope of one of India's pioneer architects. 4th Lord is in the 9th aspecting the Lagna in his own house. Another Yogakaraka Mars with Jupiter in the 9th. Budha Aditya Yoga is evident in the 10th House with Dharma Karmadhipathya Yoga. Brilliant academic and career for the individual. As we have seen earlier, the 2nd, 4th, 5th and 9th Houses and their Lords have a prominent role to play in the academic pursuits of any individual.

CHAPTER 8

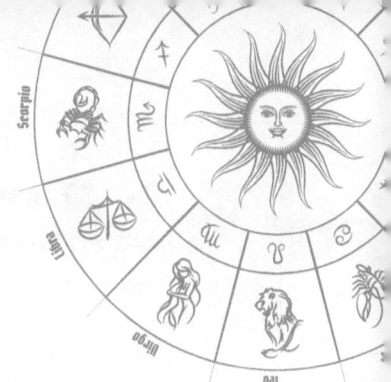

THE IMPORTANT HOUSE 10TH HOUSE

The 10th House signifies career (job, profession, business), which leads to the livelihood of individuals. The 10th House also reflects an individual's name, fame and growth prospects. It also measures how much support one gets from co-workers and family members in pursuit of Karma. The placement of the 10th Lord in one's horoscope determines one's career direction. If the 10th Lord is associated with benefics, the native will have a happy disposition. If associated with malefics, then they will be surrounded by sorrow. We shall now look at the effect of the 10th Lord placed in various Houses of your chart right from the 1st to the 12th House.

House	Traits
1	Happy disposition but willing to work hard or put in much effort in whatever one does. The native would attract name and fame. Assured of growth in the career if associated with benefics. Will maintain the right kind of relationships with co-workers.

2	Whatever career one pursues, if the 10th Lord is in the 2nd House, there will be huge income generation and wealth creation. The family would be of immense support to the natives. In all likelihood, one may pursue a family business or profession.
3	The native may be on his own since he will have courage and be an excellent communicator. He will settle for an ordinary or petty job without much means or consequences if the planet is afflicted.
4	"Work from home" slogan is meant for these people. Likely to be in real estate, automobiles, and agriculture pursuits for a career. One thing deterrent is if anything inappropriate happens in the workplace, it will directly affect the mental peace of the native.
5	Excellent career prospects, especially in one's creativity and native intelligence. They may pursue more than one business. They also will enjoy doing the work and also look for progress throughout their career. If the 10th Lord is well disposed in the House, then the native would rise up to dizzy heights. A career in the areas of engineering, law, oil and gas is a clear possibility. May pursue exploratory studies and may choose education as a career.

6	Likely to be employed with some organization. They are good at managing adverse situations and can be an excellent crisis manager. A career in the area of hospitality general service is likely. If the 10th Lord is ill-disposed, then the native will face obstacles in the workplace.
7	The person will be devoted to work. The native will also have strong relationships with people around them and will pursue business. They can communicate, engage and partner with people and will be successful in business pursuits.
8	Reflects a work generated from unknown and behind-the-scenes sources. Even Research or exploratory nature of work will suit them. Frequent change in career is very likely, especially as one ages. Relationships with people can get easily strained, and therefore, we need to be careful at work place.
9	The native will seek expansion in whatever career one pursues and will reach great heights. The native will be a thinking person and very likely to be a knowledge worker. A career in education would also be promising. Social work with people's interest would be an excellent career prospect for the native. May follow the parents' profession.

10	The native will have a very stable job and high confidence in this arrangement. Career will not be disturbed from any other source, and the growth will manifest depending on the experience. If the planet is unafflicted and with dignity, then the native will be very lucky and successful in their career. One will have the support of the government in such an arrangement. One will be assured of a high position if working in an organization and successful if in a profession or business.
11	One's aspiration and desires towards a career is likely to be fulfilled. The native enjoys high income, wealth generation and status. A career may be linked to travelling and can be an inspirational speaker. If the planet does not have dignity, relationships with people around will be difficult, and the mind will be crowded with negative thinking.
12	If the planet is well placed or with dignity, it may work in the spiritual field, travelling, voluntary organizations and abroad. May work in law enforcing agencies or in isolated places, especially does well in foreign assignments and travel-based occupations. If the planet is not well placed, then the native will suffer from losses and indulge in nefarious activities.

We have now discussed what happens if the 10th Lord is placed in the various Houses ranging from 1 to 12. Now, let us discuss the Aspects

Planets aspecting the 10th House

If Sun aspects, then success in all ventures. It might be detrimental to the native's mother.

If Moon aspects the 10th House, one will do well in the jewelry, cloth and chemical businesses.

If Mars aspects, the native will be happy and lucky. The native will derive more benefits than the efforts put in. He will also works in uniformed services.

If Mercury aspects, the native will be a creative person like an author, poet, artist, public speaker, etc. Will take up constructive efforts and likely to be highly respected.

If Jupiter aspects, he will pursue law, judiciary, government job, religion and politics as a career. He is a man with the mind for expansion and growth. He will be one with a happy and thinking disposition.

If Venus aspects, it is likely to work in the entertainment world, art and communication area. He will be blessed with a good family and a happy disposition.

If Saturn aspects, he is likely to work in mines, law enforcing agencies, and engineering and be a leader of the masses. If it isnot with dignity, then it might bring disgrace to the native. Rahu takes after Saturn, and Ketu acts like Mars.

We have now seen the 10th Lord in various Houses and the aspects of various planets on the 10th House.

Example Chart 1

		Ketu	
	Rasi		Sun Mercury
Moon			Mars
	Rahu Asc		Venus Jupiter Saturn

	Ketu Saturn		Mars
	Navamsa		Moon Asc
Venus			
	Sun	Mercury Rahu	Jupiter

Look at the 10th Lord placed in the 9th on a full moon day. Lagna Lord is placed in the 10th. These render the House of career/Karma very strong. The Lord of Lagna is placed in a benefic sign which augurs well for the native. The individual is a business tycoon. From scratch, the native made it to the riches by sheer hard work and clear thinking. Scorpio rising with the influence of Rahu, Mars, and Saturn made him an automobile manufacturer. The moon's position both in Rasi and Navamsa made him fearless and open-hearted. A unique feature of the horoscope is that the 6th, 8th and 12th Houses are free and clear without any planet. Saturn Dasa gave him riches as it is in the 11th in Rasi and 10th in Navamsa with Neechabanga. You may note that all the major planets are placed in them. The 9th, 10th and 11th Houses of the horoscope renders the native a very strong character. There is an inter relation between planets in 9, 10 and 11th Houses which shaped his company's features also.

Example Chart 2

Moon Asc		Mars	Saturn
		Rasi	Rahu Jupiter
Ketu			Venus
			Sun Mercury

10th Lord exalted in the 5th House with exchange of House. 10th Lord aspects the Lagna that sums up the entire story. This is a horoscope of a medical practitioner in the government. The 6th House has a benefic planet aspected by the 2nd and 9th Lord. The 6th Lord Sun is rendered strong by exalted 7th House Lord Mercury.

Sun and Mercury conjunction in the 7th makes the native enjoy great professional acumen and application of mind. Saturn is the 11th Lord aspecting the 6th, 10th and Lagna, a redeeming feature for professional success. In a nutshell, the 10th, 7th, 5th and 6th Houses are very strong, hence the profession's success.

CHAPTER 9

THE PIVOT (DASAMSA/ D10)

*E*veryone knows there are 12 Rasi signs. So, everyone born in a span of 2 hours in a given day are likely to have the same Lagna since there are 24 hours in a day. Many people with the same date, born within a block of 2 hours and around the same place of birth will have similar horoscopes. Consider the horoscope of twins; most of them have identical charts. Despite this, the twins do not have the same destiny. Then, how do we differentiate it for prediction?

How do we then use different predictions for each of such people? There comes into play Varga charts. To pursue astrology seriously, one must understand Varga or divisional charts.

Varga Chart Calculation

All Varga or divisional charts originate from the horoscope or chart called a Rasi chart or Dl chart. The rising degree will be used to determine the Lagna. In the same way, the degrees in which the 9 planets are placed will determine their position in the Varga Charts. According to Sage Parasara, at least 16 divisional (or) Varga charts are of importance. The 16 Divisional (or) Varga Charts reflect a particular aspect of the horoscope (or) the individual's future.

Let us see the 16 Varga (or) divisional charts and what they stand for:

S.No.	Divisional Chart	Computation/Division of Rasi
D1	Rasi	Longitude of ranges 0°-30°, totaling 12 Rasis
D2	Hora	Divided into 2 equal parts of 15° each
D3	Drekkona chart	Divided into 3 equal parts of 10 each
D4	Chaturthamsa	Divided into 4 equal parts of 7.5 each
D5	Panchamsa	Divided into 5 equal parts of 6° each
D6	Shashthamsa	Divided into 6 equal parts of 5° each
D7	Saptamsa	Divided into 7 equal parts of 4° 17' 8.57"
D8	Ashtamsa	Divided into 8 equal parts of 3° 45' each
D9	Navamsa	Divided into 9 equal parts of 3° 20'

D10	Dasamsa	Divided into 10 equal parts of 3° each
D11	Ridramsa	Divided into 11 equal parts of 2° 43'38"
D12	Dwadasamsa	Divided into 12 equal parts of 2° 30' each
D16	Shodasamsa	Divided into 16 equal parts of 1° 52' 30"
D20	Vimsamsa	Divided into 20 equal parts of 1° 30' each
D24	Chaturvimasamsa	24 equal parts of 1° 15' each
D27	Nakshatramsa	27 equal parts of 1° 6' 40" each
D30	Trimsamsa	30 equal parts of 1 degree each
D40	Khavedamsa	40 equal parts of 45' each
D45	Aksharedamsa	45 equal parts of 40' each
D60	Shastiamsa	Divided into 60 equal parts of 30' each

Significance of Divisional Charts

S.No.	Divisional Chart	Effect on the following aspect of Life
D1	Rasi	Denotes the physical and its aspects. Birth to death, general aspects at the physical level
D2	Hora	Income and Wealth
D3	Drekkona	Matters and aspects related to siblings, Accidents

D4	Chaturthamsa	Residence, properties, real estate and fortune
D5	Panchamsa	Fame, name and power
D6	Shashthamsa	Health issues
D7	Saptamsa	Related to children
D8	Ashtamsa	Accidents unexpected troubles
D9	Navamsa	Marriage and matters related to business partners, interaction with others
D10	Dasamsa	Career, achievements
D11	Ridramsa	Death and adverse events
D12	Dwadasamsa	Parents and their wellbeing and blood relatives of parents
D16	Shodasamsa	Comforts, pleasures, vehicles and discomforts
D20	Vimsamsa	Spiritual and religious matters
D24	Chaturvimasamsa	Knowledge, intelligence, education
D27	Nakshatramsa	Strengths and weakness, mental attitude, spiritual connection
D30	Trimsamsa	Evils, misfortunes and difficulties
D40	Khavedamsa	Auspicious events and properties from the maternal side
D45	Aksharedamsa	All general matters
D60	Shastiamsa	All matters and one's Karma

We can arrive at the divisional charts using astrological software or preexisting tables. Nowadays, software is easily available, which makes it all the easier to study. Apart from the above 16 divisional charts, there are some non-Parasara divisional charts which we may not give that much importance.

Normally, natal birth charts, Navamsa and Shastiamsa are ascribed or given more importance.

Dasamsa/D10 Chart

To understand career choices, change, rise, fall, growth, etc., we can look at Dasamsa.

Strength of planets in Dasamsa (or) D10 chart

A planet, when placed in its exaltation sign, in its own sign, in its friend sign, gives excellent results. It will likely give bad and sad results when placed in enemy and debilitation sign or weak. Normally, to have an overall picture, we can take into count the planet placement in all the divisional charts and come to a conclusion. If a planet is well placed in more divisional charts, it will act better and more beneficial.

How to read a Dasamsa chart

The Dasamsa/D10 chart will be treated much like a Rasi Chart or a normal birth chart. Look for Yoga's like Raja Yogas and Dhana Yogas. A greater number of Yogas will fortify the horoscope, and good results will be predicted.

The ascendant Lord of D10 chart should be well placed without any affliction for good results. A strong and unafflicted Dasamsa will give an excellent career (job, profession, business).

Some exemptions are there for D10 Chart. The placement of Mercury in the 8th and Mars in the 6th is considered good.

The Dasa period is also important. Dasa of a strong planet in Dasamsa will give excellent results.

If a planet is in Dusthana 6,8,12 in the natal chart and D10 chart, it gives bad results.

Rules for Vargottama, debilitation, combustion and planetary war of planets remain the same for D10, just like the Natal Chart. Planets in the 3rd or 8th of Dasamsa or D10 Chart will not give good results. Atmakaraka and Amatyakaraka, as per the Jaimini system, should be well placed in the D10 Chart to bring good fortune.

After analyzing the D1 and D10 Charts, we will clearly understand one's job/career/profession. All the material benefits could be read by analyzing the natal chart, Navamsa and Dasamsa or D10 Chart.

Indicators

D10 Chart indicates the Karma in the present birth. Karma will encompass all the activities undertaken by an individual daily. A doctor may do social work and could be a politician too. The D10 Chart will reflect the nature of all the individual's activities. The Trikonas, namely 2nd, 6th and 10th, are very important for the

assessment of income, employment, career, growth, etc. We will be discussing this aspect in detail in another section of this book.

Various Houses of D10 Chart

- The 1st House indicates our willingness to perform.
- The 2nd House has got to do with income generation and wealth creation.
- The 3rd House indicates courage, communication, siblings, support, change and travel.
- The 4th House indicates happiness.
- The 5th House indicates native intelligence, our subordination, creativity, etc.
- The 6th House indicates the will to face challenges and obstacles and the ability to avail loans.
- Malefic planets in the 6th House of D10 Charts always is good.
- The 7th House indicate business and relationship with co-workers
- The 8th House indicates obstacles, sudden upsets and generally unfavourable results
- The 9th House indicates one's luck (or) fortune. It also stands for your bosses.

Therefore, the 9th House in the D10 chart assumes considerable importance

- The 10th House is the most important one, indicating the Karma in present life.

It signifies growth, rise and fame in whatever endeavor an individual undertakes and it clearly indicates success in all ventures.

- The 11th House generally indicates gain in all efforts. They will have the support of elder siblings.

- The 12th House stands for loss and general weakness that a person would suffer from.

We have discussed D10 charts in brief, and we will devote some time to studying examples of D1 and D10 charts elsewhere in the book.

Dasamsa

Example Chart 1

		Sun Mercury Ketu Asc	Venus Mars
Saturn			
Jupiter	Rasi		
	Rahu	Moon	

	Mercury Asc	Jupiter Moon	Saturn
Venus	Dasamsa		Rahu
Ketu			Mars
			Sun

This is the horoscope of an industrialist. Taurus is rising with the 2nd, 4th and 5th Lord in conjunctions, giving rise to Dhana Yoga. It is a good sign; the native would look for gains throughout his life. Moon in the 6th House makes one bold in decision making. Yogakaraka Saturn occupying the 11th is an excellent placement for material benefit and peace of mind. Jupiter in 10th with Parivarthana Yoga makes one develop a good code of conduct and integrity.

Dasamsa has Saturn in 3rd, which is a welcome position. Exalted 4th Lord Moon with 9th Lord Jupiter forms an important Dhana Yoga and Gajakesari Yoga. Jupiter aspects the 10th House in Dasamsa. Lagna Lord in 5th makes the native intelligent, balanced and practically wise. The native thoroughly enjoyed Mercury/Ketu and Venus Dasas.

Dasamsa has excellent placements, and the industrialist did well for himself and society.

Example Chart 2

This is also a horoscope of an industrialist who restructured his family business and opened new avenues.

Saturn	Rahu	Sun Mercury	
			Jupiter Venus Asc
	Rasi		Moon
		Ketu	Mars

Saturn			Jupiter Asc
			Rahu Venus
Ketu Mercury	Dasamsa		
Mars		Sun Moon	

Born in an emotional sign, the placement of Jupiter made the native a well-balanced and deep-thinking personality. A conjunction of the 4th and 9th Lord forms a strong Dhana Yoga.

Lagna Lord in 2nd, which is a friendly placement, augurs well for wealth since the 2nd Lord itself is in the 11th. Yogakaraka aspects the 9th, which is a blessing.

Dasamsa again has Jupiter in Lagna, aspecting the 5th, 7th and 9th, enabling business. 2nd Lord is in 5th aspected by Jupiter. 6th and 11th Lord Mars in a Kendra aspected by Jupiter.

So, it is evident that we need to have a well-placed Dasamsa to succeed in professional endeavours. Many people do not read Dasamsa, but it becomes crucial when the birth chart does not give a clear indication.

CHAPTER 10

NAVAMSA -D9

The previous chapter discussed Varga charts and Dasamsa (D10). The ancient classical texts do not contain much information on interpreting Varga charts. We must also note that there is much talk about the Navamsa chart in most ancient astrological works. The Navamsa is called a 'twin chart' or 'queen of charts.' Rasi and Navamsa are king and queen in the chart interpretation.

How to calculate Navamsa

It need not trouble us since software is available to simplify the work. Calculation is easy as tabulations are also available, and without knowing degrees, we can arrive at Navamsa. We read the Navamsa chart to ascertain three aspects:

a) The strength of planets and it also gets reflected in Shadbala calculations
b) To ascertain the success of marriage
c) To ascertain the career, success, growth, fall, obstacles, etc.

A brief on how the Navamsa chart is reckoned. Navamsa is best understood as the 9th part of 30° degrees in a Rasi.

300/9 = 3° 20"

Each Navamsa part will be 3° 20". We can decide the Rasi's into moving, fixed and common signs. We have a tabulation by which the planets placed in the Rasi can be redistributed to the various Navamsas. Since the software is available, we need not bother about details.

One Rasi will have approximately a 2-hour time period or otherwise 120 minutes. So, in the case of twins, the Navamsa can show a marked difference. Navamsa reading will make a world of difference for people born in the same Lagna, same day and place.

Navamsa chart reading can be similar to a Rasi Chart in Vedic astrology. If a planet is well placed in Rasi and Navamsa, it gives excellent results. For example, if Mercury is exalted in Virgo for a Kanya Lagna native and also in Navamsa, then it gives excellent results. The placement of the planet both in the same Rasi and Navamsa goes by the name Vargottama. Of course, it need not be good always.

Generally, Vargottama is considered good if the planet is benefic and well-placed to Lagna. If an exalted planet in Rasi becomes debilitated in Navamsa, it may not auger well for the native. Dasa of such a planet will always be detrimental to the native. If some aspect is complex to read in Rasi, then it can be clearly interpreted with the help of a Navamsa chart.

Jaimini's method of astrology deals at length with the interpretation of the Navamsa chart for better understanding. The placement of Atma Karaka is of utmost importance. The strength of Amatya Karaka will determine the career status of the native. Those interested in studying Jaimini's method should keep this point in mind. This sign of Atma Karaka is also called Karakamsa in Jaimini's method, and that should be reckoned as a Lagna, which will reveal a lot about the native.

12 Houses in Navamsa (or) D9 Chart

House	Traits
1	Overall health and the longevity of the spouse
2	Wealth creation, income generation and family status/welfare
3	Courage, communication, efforts to sustain a marriage, short travel regarding work or business
4	Profession of one's spouse. Education and general happiness of that native. Income through conveyance, estate in general. The House also shows a change in profession of the native and spouse.
5	Creativity, intelligence and its application in their job, profession and business. Happiness in conjugal life also comes out.
6	Debt accumulated through business or one's life in general
7	Reflects the native's business acumen and the partners' strength in business. It reveals the strength and support of the peers if one is employed.
8	This House is one of mystery and uncertainties in one's life, which affects an individual's career.

9	Indicates the boss and the individual's skill sets, which will strengthen one's career. It also has to do with luck, positive thinking, and higher studies, especially of exploratory nature.
10	Reflects one's Karma, what one does to earn his living. This House also reflects the application of mind, integrity, hard work, and rise in career status. A strong 10th Lord and 10th House will take the native to a greater height.
11	Denotes the individual's desires, hopes and aspirations, without which one cannot come up in life. Also indicates gains and material benefits.
12	Indicates losses, energy spent, and litigation in connection with one's career. Also indicates foreign travel related to one's occupation.

The main Houses to analyse in Navamsa (D9) are the 1st, 2nd, 6th, 9th, 10th and 11th for understanding an individual's career. The individual's inherent physical and mental strength from the 1st House and the 6th House indicates how a native faces adversary and remains calm. The 9th House can make choices and use opportunities. The 10th House is the actual effort, application of mind and physical energy in a job/business/profession. The 10th House of the D9 chart also gives knowledge about the career. We get a clear picture through the strength of the 10th House, conjunctions, and the 10th House Lord. The 10th House of D9 Chart also indicates the specific profession one would undertake. If more than one planet is posited in the 10th House of D9 Chart, then it is beneficial to the native and will strengthen his Karmic force.

If only one planet is placed in the 10th House of the D9 Chart having a connection with the 1st or 2nd House of the Chart, then the native is likely to pursue an independent business or profession.

10th House when connected with 6th and 2nd House indicates job/employment. To come up in employment, one needs a strong 6th House to manage people effectively and a strong 2nd House to generate adequate income. In net effect, the 10th ruling planet should be in conjunction with the 6th and 2nd lord or associated with aspects for successful employment.

When the 10th House of D9 Chart connects with the 7th and 2nd Lord, it indicates business, mostly in consumer goods.

Therefore, the 10th House in the Navamsa chart can be employed to study the precise nature and characteristics of one's livelihood. What skill set that the native will possess, and how well will it be employed in a career or profession?

NAVAMSA

Example Chart 1

Mercury Rahu	Rasi	Moon Jupiter
Sun		Ketu
Asc Mars Venus	Saturn	

			Sun Venus Saturn
Moon	Navamsa		Mars Ketu
Rahu			
		Jupiter Mercury	Asc

Sagittarius Lagna with Lord exalted in conjunction with the moon, forming Gajakesari Yoga. Thus, the Lagna becomes strong and adds value to the chart. 5th Lord Mars, in conjunction with 11th Lord Venus in Lagna and associated with the Sun in Navamsa, is an excellent formation for Dhana Yoga. Since the Lagna Lord is strong and the 2nd Lord is exalted in the 11th, it makes the native independent and progressive.

Mars' association with Venus gave him estates and vehicles. The native had a humble beginning because of Adhama Yoga. Navamsa has benefics in 2nd House. Mercury's conjunction with Jupiter gives rise to Dhana Yoga. 10th House Sun, Venus and Saturn augur well for his growth since Saturn and Venus are Yogakarakas for Navamsa Lagna.

Example Horoscope 2

		Ketu	Jupiter
Moon	Rasi		
Asc			Saturn
	Mars Rahu	Mercury	Sun Venus

		Jupiter Saturn	
Rahu	Navamsa		Venus Asc
Moon			Ketu
Mars		Mercury	Sun

Saturn becomes Lagna Lord and Rasi Lord and aspects Moon. In Navamsa, benefic Venus in Lagna aspected by Lagna Lord Moon. It is a great arrangement and a strong Lagna. Due to the above Navamsa deposition, the native was good-looking and slightly built.

Sun in 9th make the native balanced in outlook. The Exchange of Houses by Mercury and Venus renders strength to the horoscope. The exchange makes the native precise in detail, hardworking and courteous, bringing him progressive success throughout his life. The Putrakarka has been rendered strong in navamsa, and therefore, the native had a good number of children. Saturn Dasa favoured the native with financial stability, although a delicate health. It is important to study the Navamsa also for ascertaining one's career/profession and general wellbeing.

CHAPTER 11

IMPORTANCE OF PLANETS IN 10TH HOUSE

*T*he Tenth House plays an important role in ascertaining one's career/profession. We have already discussed this in an earlier chapter while covering the 10th House, Dasamsa and Navamsa. We will now discuss the effects of different planets in the 10th House. All nine planets can be in the 10th House for any Lagna. So, the permutation/combination for predictions will be cumbersome to list out in this book. We will examine the significance of planets if placed in the 10th House identical to their own or exaltation. More or less, one will get the same type of benefits with some varying degrees in other than ruling House.

If planets are placed in the 10th House, which are inimical or debilitated, the results will be disastrous for the native. If there are compensating factors, then there will be redemption. The benefit will be manifold if one has an exalted planet in the 10th House.

Lagnas Cancer, Libra, Sagittarius, Capricorn, Aries and Gemini will have this benefit. So, if a planet is ruling or exalted in the 10th place, then the native stands to benefit throughout his life. The native's growth will be phenomenal and will increase with age provided if there are no hindering arrangements. Remember that the 6th, 8th and 12th Lord should not be in the 10th House.

The impact of 10th House planets are:

Sun in 10th House

- It is a great blessing if the Sun is found in the 10th House with good dignity. For example, Lord Rama had an exalted Sun in the 10th in Aries. It indicates the impact that a 10th House Sun can signify. Of course, there are several other parameters like Lordship, in which Nakshatra Pada falls, placement in Varga charts, etc. The Sun in the 10th House is a unique position for any chart.
- Vedic astrology says that the Sun is the most important planet and supreme in nature. The Sun represents one's soul and the energy that the soul releases. It also marks distinct characters for each individual.
- The 10th House is one of the strongest Houses in the chart, and almost all planets give good results in the 10th House. Sun attains Digbala and is with utmost strength in the 10th House. It gets directional strength.

	Sun		
			Asc
	Rasi		

- Sun in the 10th House makes an individual well-educated, aspiring, hardworking and courageous. It makes one intelligent and worldly wise.
- Sun will take an individual to the top echelons of government. They will be bestowed with great support. The placement of the Sun is important when someone works or is associated with the government.
- It brings success in education especially when associated with Mercury.
- If one has a debilitated Sun in the 10th House as in Capricorn Lagna, then there will be disastrous results unless there is Neecha Banga Rajo Yoga, which will be redeeming.
- For one born in Aries, Cancer, Scorpio, Sagittarius and Leo, a 10th House Sun will bring in very good effects and benefits.

Moon in the 10th House

- Moon in 10th House will get a native associated with hospitality, hotel and water-born products/industries.
- Moon is also linked to travel industry.

		Moon
	Rasi	
	Asc	

- Moon stands for the emotional responses of an individual. It signifies mind, and therefore, a strong Moon will bestow balance of mind.
- Moon will also bring in authority and government support.
- It can make one a diplomat in a foreign land.
- They will enjoy support and encouragement from their mother. They will be a big support to the family and will be a guiding light.
- One will be highly literate, scholarly and intelligent.
- May rise from a poor household to become a successful businessman.
- If Moon is rendered weak, then the native will suffer from a weak body, difficult childhood, ups and downs in business and will face obstacles.

Jupiter in the 10th House

Jupiter is called a planet of expansions and bestows all good benefits to the native if placed with dignity. Its aspect brings even better results.

- When Jupiter is in the 10th House, the native assumes responsibility.
- They will get the support of all around in all their endeavours.
- Success in business and social work is assured.

Asc			
	Rasi		
Jupiter			

- They are to be trusted and dependable in all circumstances. Their reliability makes them fit for people-related jobs or where leadership qualities are necessary.
- Natives with well-placed Jupiter are endowed with the ability to see the future and are intuitive.
- They can be egoistic sometimes and will not be accommodative, which is a negative trait.
- Jupiter stands for expansion and growth, so when Jupiter is in 10th, it guarantees success.

Venus in 10 House

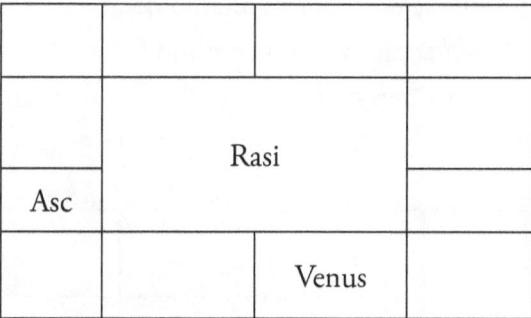

- Venus represents love, affection, beauty and emotions. So, wherever the 10th House Venus is found, the native will have the right balance of the above.
- The native is sociable and excellent in network and interpersonal relationships.
- 10th house Venus of the native will make the spouse get associated with one's professional efforts.
- Their arrangement will make one work in the motor industry, hospitals, hotels, computer allied, art and artefact industry, milk industry, ornamental industry, wellbeing health products and judiciary.

Mars in the 10th House

- The placement of Mars in the 10th house is a beneficial placement to have. The malefic planets become strong since the 10th House is a Kendra and Upachya House. Mars in classical texts stands for war, fiery element and action.
- It makes one courageous, daredevil, hardworking and action-oriented.

- It can give progress, prosperity and wellbeing.
- They will gain directional strength in the 10th House and, therefore, will be powerful enough to do good.
- They will gain appreciation, name and fame.
- They can sometimes become quarrelsome and aggressive.
- They give rise to professional interest in the area of real estate.

	Asc		
		Rasi	
Mars			

- 10th House Mars in Scorpio makes one a doctor.
- Mars, in conjunction with Mercury, makes one an engineer.
- Other than the moon and Sun, Mars also enables one to get a government job.
- Mars in the 10th will be a blessing for Leo and Pisces ascendant. In the case of Cancer and Leo Lagna, it becomes a Yogakaraka and therefore bestows good results.
- Talented, competent government jobs, managing charitable trusts and all the uniformed services will be in the purview of such people.

Mercury in the 10th House

- Mercury in 10th House is an excellent placement, giving rise to excellent career, dignity and professional acumen. The 10th House Mercury is related to communication, accounting, publishing and engineering. The native does an excellent network job and, therefore, is competent to hold leadership positions in the organization.

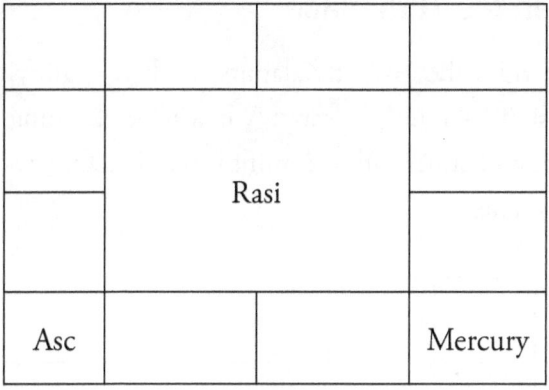

- May lead to government jobs
- Gains through parents
- Intelligent and analytical in nature and therefore good for exploratory jobs
- Has excellent skill sets for authoring books, blogs, etc. and can be an editor and publisher
- Eloquent in speech and might turn out to be a public speaker, teacher, etc.
- Can turn out to be an entrepreneur
- Develops skill sets for a mathematician and accountant
- Effective in general administration and, therefore, effective in the corporate world

- Can have a balance of mind and be effective in arguments and consequently an effective lawyer. If supported by Jupiter, then the native can become a judge.
- One can become respected, sociable and famous
- Will take up a business, agency, mathematician, accountant, teacher, auditor, printing, media, engineer and communication type of jobs

Saturn in the 10th place

- Saturn rules the 10th of Kalapursha Chart, signifying career/profession in multiple ways. We will be devoting an entire chapter on Saturn and its significance. Therefore, we will limit ourselves here.

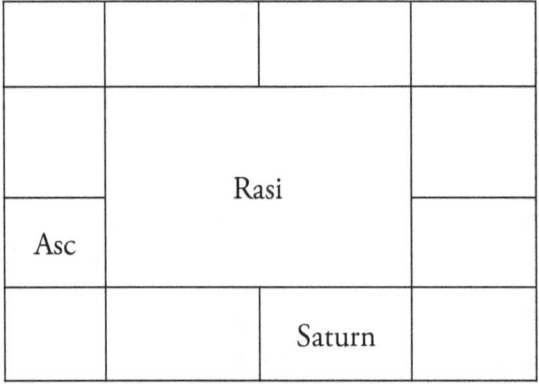

- Saturn is often misunderstood as the most malefic planet, but the reality is if the planet is with dignity, it can bring forth excellent positive results.
- Saturn signifies hard work, discipline, justice, and serving the masses, the poor and under privileged.

- It also signifies serious difficult, obstacles, and permanent aspects.
- If the 10th House is Capricorn, Aquarius, or Libra, they produce very progressive results.
- These natives will receive favours from the government.
- Native will be associated with mines, metallurgy, paints, jails, law enforcing agencies, leather goods, fuel, police and water management.

Rahu in the 10th House

Rahu will be more effective if it is placed in the 10th House. In fact, it is the best House for Rahu. It brings in name, fame, material benefits, extensive travelling and luxury.

		Rahu	
	Rasi		
			Asc

- They will be a success in the fields of software technology, media and entertainment.
- Can take up unconventional work that is not routine. Therefore, they are fit to take up research and exploratory work.
- Strong Rahu can make a person affluent within a short time.

- A combination of Rahu and Venus will give exceptionally good results.
- If Rahu is weak in the 10th House, it can bring misery, hurdles, obstacles and defamation.
- If afflicted, it can make a native sick or unhealthy.

Ketu in the 10th House

- Ketu's position in the 10th is not a welcome feature, although some good results may come along the way.
- Ketu's insecurity in the 10th place may give hardships, restlessness, and dogmatic thinking.
- Work-life balance for such people may be affected. Care should be taken to balance it out if Ketu is in the 10th House.
- The native can be intelligent with an ability to solve problems and mysteries and therefore, can be engaged with jobs associated with it.

Asc	Rasi		
	Ketu		

- If well placed, Ketu can bring in financial wealth, expansion in general life and will be held in high esteem by the people around.

Generally, it is not useful for trade and business, and therefore, people with Ketu in 10th place should prefer a job/employment.

CHAPTER 12

TIMING IN PROFESSION

The timing of events is a difficult and tricky job for astrologers. Several factors are associated with the field of profession, and hence, timing is very difficult. The most important houses are the 2nd House of income, 9th House of fortune and 10th House of profession. In the Varga charts, Dasamsa reveals the profession of the individuals. The strength of the 10th lord in the D-10 chart and the Lagna lord of the D-10 chart should be given equal importance.

For the timing of events, it is advisable to follow Vimshotri Dasa. The Dasa factors to be considered are as follows:

1. Dasa of the 10th Lord
2. Dasa of the disposition of the 10th Lord
3. Lagna lord of the D-10 chart
4. Planets in conjunction with the 10th lord
5. Dasa of the 7th lord

In addition to these Dasas, we need to consider the transit of major planets Saturn and Jupiter. Saturn will do well in the 3rd, 6th and 11th on transits from the moon. Jupiter will do well in the 2nd, 5th, 7th, 9th and 11th.

The transits should have a benefic association with the 10th House, 10th lord, 7th House and 7th Lord.

If the Dasas, as mentioned above, happen, and the transit parameters are satisfactory, the native will be able to succeed in the profession or get a favourable change.

Example chart – 1

Ketu Jupiter Moon	Rasi		Venus Rahu
Saturn			Asc Sun Mercury Mars

In the year 2013, in Jupiter, Dasa the native got the crucial elevation to a top post in a government of India undertaking. Please note Jupiter is the 7th lord aspecting the 10th lord, which gave the native a meaningful elevation. Mars, in conjunction with the 10th Lord, is in exaltation. Jupiter was also transiting on the 11th from Lagna and the 7th from the moon sign. In the same way, the native also got a favourable transfer during that period of Saturn/Mercury Dasa. Mercury is the 10th lord, and Saturn is the 10th Lord in the natal chart. Jupiter was transiting the 2nd from Lagna and 10th from the moon sign.

During both occasions, the Dasa and the transit were very favourable to the native and hence the events. Similarly, it would be best if you kept in mind the different dasa factors and transit to time the events appropriately.

Example Chart: 2

Asc		Rahu	
Jupiter	Rasi		Saturn
Mars	Venus Ketu	Sun Moon	Mercury

The Sun, Moon and Mars Bhukthis in Mercury Dasa saw him as United States Commander in Europe, as Supreme Commander for Allied Forces and also clinched Victory in the Second World War (1939-1945). The mercury dasa was an extraordinary period for the native. Mercury stands exalted in the 7th aspected by Jupiter. Since it was a Pancha Maga Purusha Yoga, the native garnered name and fame. In this case, we also see the influence of the 7th and 10th Lords taking the native to a magnificent stature in his political career, which resulted in him becoming the president of the United States of America.

DASA BHUKTHI RULES

- The Dasa of Lord of Lagna has an excellent career associated with the 5th Lord.
- The association between Lord of Lagna and the 10th house gives excellent results in their Dasas and Bhukthis.
- The Dasa of the 10th Lord, when associated with the 5th Lord, gives rise to excellent results. In the same way, if the Lord of the 4th House is associated with the 5th Lord, one can expect the same good results.
- If the 10th Lord is placed in 9th, during its dasa, it will give the native name, fame and wealth in the chosen Profession.
- Dasas of Yogakaraka, Kona and Trikona Lords augur well for the profession.
- If the Lord of Lagna is strong and placed in the 10th, its Dasa will bring prosperity throughout the Dasa.
- The Dasas of the 2nd and 12th Lord will be neutral in outcome. If the 2nd Lord is well placed with dignity, predict riches in its Dasa.
- Saturn Dasa gives good results for Rishaba, Mithuna, Kanya, Thulam, Makaram and Kumbam, if well-placed with dignity. However, there could be a success after a bit of effort.
- Lords of 1st, 5th and 9th give good results during their Dasas provided they are with dignity and well placed, even if they are malefic.

- Lords of 3rd, 6th and 11th give bad results. There may be some material benefits during the dasa of the 11th Lord.
- Lord of 8th house dasa gives bad or evil results.
- Lord of 4th, 5th and 10th houses, if they are placed in any one of these houses, then such Dasa will give excellent results if they are functional benefics.
- The Dasa of the planet associated with Lords of 1st, 5th and 10th can give riches provided the planet is a functional benefic.
- During the 10th Lord Dasa, if it is with dignity, there will be a success in all endeavors for the native.
- The Dasa of the planets, when combined with the 10th Lord, even if it is a malefic, may give rise to good results.
- If the exchange between the 9th & 10th Lord, then its Dasas will give riches, success and fame.
- In the same way, if there is any exchange between the 5th and 10th Lord, the Dasas will give name and fame to the native.
- If the Dasa/Bhukthi planets are in mutual Kendras or Konas to each other, then predict good results regarding such Bhukthis.
- Planet rulership of 1st, 4th, 5th, 9th and 10th are supposed to yield good results during their Dasas if placed with dignity.

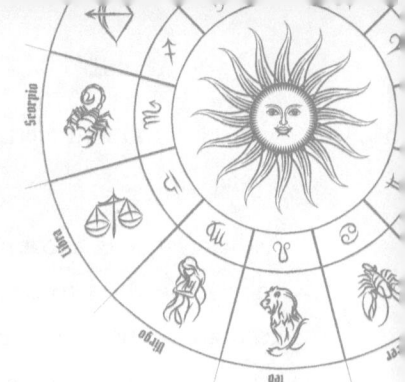

CHAPTER 13

ASTHAKAVARGA AND PROFESSION

*T*here are very many predictive techniques in Vedic astrology. Parasara and, later, Varamibra fine-tuned the Asthakavarga system of prediction. The advent of software made it easy to structure and interpret the Asthakavarga chart for predictions. This system should be used in integration with other tools of Vedic astrology. This system not only takes care of the analysis of Rasi and Varga charts but is also helpful in interpreting the Dasa system and Gochara.

In the Asthakavarga Chart, each planet is considered to be bestowing a benefic impact on certain Rasis from its own Rasi position in the natal Chart and corresponding to other planets' placement or position. There is nothing to worry about now as the computer handles the laborious calculations. This system also makes us understand the negative and positive effects of the planets. Rahu and Ketu do not play a role, but Lagna does play a role.

Asthakavarga is a complex system that astrologers do not use widely. Needless to say, with this system, predictions are more accurate. Usually, planets in their own Rasi, Moolatrikona (or) exaltation are strong, but if the Rasi in which they are placed has less than 28 dots, they do not give benefic results. For each of the Houses, there is a minimum number of dots required, and they are as below.

House Number	Dots
1	25
2	22
3	29
4	24
5	25
6	34
7	19
8	24
9	29
10	36
11	54
12	16

If the above minimum dots are not available in a particular House, then that House will not be strong. If the Houses have more than the minimum requirement, then that House will give positive results.

1. The 10th House from Lagna, Sun or moon, whichever has the most number of dots, will determine the course of one's career.
2. The planet that has contributed to the dots in the 10th House should be noted. Combusted and debilitated planets will not be effective anyway.
3. The dots in the 11th also count since the aspirations, desires and material benefits accrue from the 11th House.
4. If the dots from the Dasa Lord are high in the 11th, then greater will be the success in the Dasa time.
5. If a House has more dots, then the native enjoys the benefit of the House.

Example Chart 1
SARVASTHAKAVARGA

23	25	25	40
Ketu 28			Venus 39
Moon Jupiter 23	Rasi		Rahu 20
Saturn 26	34	28	Asc Sun Mars Mercury 26

Detailed Dots

Planets	Lagna	10th House	11th House
Sun	4	7	6
Moon	1	6	6
Jupiter	6	5	6
Saturn	2	7	5
Venus	5	1	5
Mercury	5	7	5
Mars	3	7	6

If we analyse the Asthakavarga, Lagna has 26 dots, the 10th has 40, and the 11th has 39. This is an excellent position for a successful career. The Lagna and 10th Lord Mercury is exalted in Lagna with 7 dots in the 10th and 5 dots in the 1st and 11th.

The native had an excellent career and retired as a director of a government of India undertaking.

The 11th Lord is in the 5th aspecting the 11th with 6 dots in the 10th House and 6 dots in the 11th House. The native is very intelligent and creative, which took him to great heights in service. Jupiter gets Neechabanga contributing 6, 5, 6 dots to Lagna, the 10th and the 11th House, respectively. The native has more dots in Lagna, 10th and 11th. The 5th House has less than the required dots. So, the native was deprived of progeny. In the same way, the Dasa of Jupiter was dreadful because of the 23 dots in Capricorn where it is placed.

Example Chart 2

23	26 Rahu	30	30
24	Rasi		28
24			Asc Saturn 26
Sun Mars Jupiter Mercury 23	27 Venus	43 Ketu	33 Moon

For Leo Lagna, the presence of Jupiter, Sun, and Mars in the 5th House is an excellent combination. The 2nd and 11th Lord in the 5th is also welcome. Because of the Asthakavarga of the D10 chart, there was a setback in his business. Mars Bhinnashtakavarga in the D10 Chart is "0" in Capricorn, which was the culprit. The setback happened in Mars Dasa when Saturn was transiting. Apart from the Rasi chart, this system is also to be given importance.

So, the Asthakavarga system is useful in analysing the natal chart, Varga chart, Dasa and transit. If one is baffled about understanding the nature of events while reading Rasi and Varga Charts, the Ashtakavarga system becomes valuable.

CHAPTER 14

EXCERPTS FROM CLASSICAL TEXT

S ome of the Classical Texts throw light on the area of profession. Although there are many inputs, let us have a contemporary understanding of a few vital inputs.

A) SARAVALI

- The 10th House counted from Lagna and Moon is called Karmasthana, and if these Lords are strong, one will prosper in their profession. Otherwise the reverse will happen.
- Effects of planets in the 10th House from Moon
  a) Sun will give success in all undertakings.
  b) Moon means a wealthy person.
  c) Mars means indulging in valorous deeds.
  d) Mercury will make one learned and wealthy.
  e) Jupiter, then one, will be righteous and affluent and have the government's favour.
  f) Venus means good-looking, fortunate and famous.

g) Saturn in the 10th will give rise to grief and poverty and make you feel emotional.

- Conjunction of planets at the 10th
  a) Sun and Mars are labourers.
  b) Sun and Mercury will be rich and be a trader.
  c) Sun and Jupiter will be brave and famous.
  d) Sun and Venus will make you dear to the people and ruling class and also wealthy.
  e) Sun and Saturn will lead to hardship, imprisonment, poverty and misery.

Likewise, you have certain predictions for a combination of other planets.

- Malefic in the 10th from the moon makes one a doctor. Aspected by a benefic, then a religious teacher. Of course, this will happen only when the moon and Saturn have dignity.
- Malefics in the 3rd or 6th from ascendant/moon will prove favourable, while in Lagna, 8th and 12th, they will be inauspicious.
- The strongest 10th from Lagna/Moon will indicate the nature of the profession.
- The Sun in the 10th means income through the father, the moon means from the mother, Mars means from the enemies, Mercury means from friends, Jupiter means from kith and kin, Venus means from the opposite gender, and Saturn means from servants.
- There will be gains in many ways if the Lagna, the 2nd and 11th are occupied by favourable planets.

- The author talks about planets and professions. Since we have discussed that in the book elsewhere, we are not covering that part.

B) JATHAGA ALANKARAM

- If Saturn is in the 4th, then the native understands the realities. If Saturn is in the 10th, he goes on a pilgrimage.
- Lagna Lord in the 10th House gives rise to success in the profession.
- If the 10th Lord is a benefic and placed in 2,9,11 and Kendras, the native will have righteous ways to do business.
- If Aries, Taurus, or Leo happen to be the 10th House and if a benefic is placed in it, the native will earn success in all ventures.
- The strongest 10th Lord from Lagna/Moon/Sun will determine the nature of business.
- The Strongest 10th Lord from Lagna/Moon/Sun, if placed in the House of Mars in Navamsa, means that the native will deal with metals.
- The Strongest 10th Lord from Lagna/Moon/Sun if placed in a Jupiter House in Navamsa, indicates that the native will do pious work.
- If in Venus Navamsa, then they will deal in Silver and jewelry will be the business.
- If in Saturn Navamsa, then ordinary physical work and will not have riches.
- If the 10th Lord is associated with the Sun and moon, the native enjoys the support of the Government.
- If the 10th Lord is associated with Mercury, then it will benefit from the opposite gender.

- If associated with Sun, then becomes a teacher, religiously oriented and will be in elite government jobs.
- If associated with Venus, then benefit through cattle in today's parlance, motor and jewellery.
- Being associated with Saturn is not linked to desirable jobs.
- If associated with Mars, then land-related.
- If the 2nd Lord, 11th and 9th is Mars, then the native will be associated with people of his liking
- If it happens to be Mercury, then progress through education and benefit through vehicles
- If it is Jupiter, then through his children.
- If it is Venus, then it is from the landed property.
- If it is Saturn, they will be in low-yielding jobs.
- If the 11th Lord is exalted in conjunction with benefics then the native will be gainfully placed.
- If the 11th Lord is in his own house or exalted, then the native will be happy and attain name and fame.
- If the depositor of the 11th Lord is in 1,4,7 or 10, the native will have gains and wealth creation.
- If the Sun happens to be the 11th Lord, and in conjunction with the moon, then the native enjoys gains.
- If Moon happens to be the 11th Lord aspected by Jupiter, then the native enjoys full satisfaction in life.

C) PHALADEEPIKA

- If there are or more planets in their own sign and exaltation, then the native will be equal to a king.
- If a planet is retrograde and does not combust, then the native will be equal to a king.

- If two or more planets attain Digbala, especially the Sun or moon, then the native enjoys Raja Yoga.
- When Lagna and Moon are in Vargottama and aspected by four planets, then the native enjoys Raja Yoga.
- If the Lord of the Lagna is in Vargottama and is posited in Kendra or Trikona in **its own sign or exaltation, then the native becomes a king.**
- **If Mars is placed in Aries and aspected by a benefic planet, then the native becomes a king.**
- Saturn is capable of conferring Raja Yoga if it were to rise with ascendant signs of Libra, Sagittarius, Capricorn and Aquarius.
- If Moon attains Vargottama and is aspected by a strong planet, the native becomes a king.
- If the benefics, namely Jupiter, Mercury and Venus, are posited in the 9th with brilliant rays, then the native becomes a king.
- If Jupiter and Moon are in a Kendra aspected by Venus, then the native becomes a king.

NEECHA BHANGA RAJA YOGA

- The Lord of the debilitated sign or the planet that is exalted in the sign should be in a Kendra from Lagna or Moon.
- The Lord of the sign of debilitation and the lord of the exaltation sign or the debilitated planet should be in mutual Kendra.
- If the planet is in its own sign of debilitation and is in a Kendra from the moon or Lagna.

There are various other Raja Yogas mentioned in Phaladeepika. Still, the above are useful in understanding the strength of the horoscope vis-a-vis the profession and also life in general.

D) SATYASAMHITA

- When the Lord of the 10th house is placed in Lagna or combination with the Lagna Lord, there will be riches and fame in its Dasa.
- If the Lord of the 10th house is placed in the 2nd house, its Dasa will generate much income and wealth.
- When the 10th Lord is in the 3rd house, the native will be courageous during its dasa.
- If the 10th Lord is posited in the 4th house, then during its Dasa, the native will be happy.
- The Dasa of the 10th Lord, when in the 5th, gives political success and forms a benefic yoga.
- The Dasa of the 10th Lord, when in 6th, gives success in litigation.
- If the 10th Lord is in the 7th and marriage happens in its Dasa, then the spouse will be from a respectable family.
- The Dasa of the 10th Lord, when placed in the 8th, will give rise to evil deeds.
- The Dasa of the 10th Lord, when placed in the 9th, gives rise to Raja Yoga with fame and riches.
- When the 10th Lord is placed in the 12th, the Dasa will bring forth expenses, obstacles, and listless travel. The 10th Lord will get afflicted if it is in the 12th house.

CHAPTER 15

SIGNIFICATOR OR KARAKA

*I*n the Kalapursha Chart, Saturn becomes the Lord of 10th House. Generally, it Saturn is perceived as a significator (or) Karaka for 6th, 8th, 10th & 12th Houses. Saturn is also a pure beneficial or Yogakaraka planet for Taurus and Libra ascendents, where Saturn becomes a Lord of Kona and Kendra. We need to study 6th & 10th house for the profession.

People normally think Saturn only does bad things to them throughout their lives. Saturn can also be a benefic under many combinations and placements. It all depends on the birth time or Lagna and the placement of Saturn in various Houses.

Saturn rules Capricorn and Aquarius, exalted in Libra and debilitated in Aries. The Houses owned by the Sun and moon, i.e., Cancer and Leo, fall for Saturn. Saturn is nearly 700 times in size when compared to the Earth, with multiple satellites and gaseous rings. Saturn takes 2½ years to move across a Rasi and approximately 29½ years to revolve around the Sun.

Saturn Attributes

Good Attributes: Makes a person disciplined, hardworking and industrious. It enables a person to care for his health and keeps one fit. Saturn makes a person form opinions, impressions and a singular mode of thinking. He hates crimes and does not go after material benefits. It gives a person mental strength and resilience to face obstacles and hardships and builds inner strength. The good effect of the planet can make one a philosopher and a social reformer.

Bad Attributes:

Saturn's ill effects can make one physically and mentally challenged or deformed. They may be plagued with diseases, distress, humiliation, misunderstanding, and poverty. When influenced, it may exhibit anger and stubbornness. Ultimately,

Saturn's placement, aspects and conjunctions will determine the effects of it on the individual.

The Houses

Now, we will see what will be the effect of Saturn on Houses like 2nd, 6th, 9th, 10th and 11th, which will have a bearing on the career of an individual.

House	Trait
2	If placed in this House, the native has to work hard and will earn less wages. The earnings will not be commensurate with the labour that one puts in. There will be a beneficial effect if Saturn is in its own House and exaltation. Usually, it is not desirable to have Saturn in the 2nd House since things promised generally are delayed or denied.
6	It gives an individual the courage to face obstacles and difficult situations in life. Therefore, they can work efficiently even in hostile or adverse situations. It helps a native to raise loans and successfully service them. Generally, a malefic planet in the 6th House is welcome. If Saturn is afflicted, then it suffers from debts and enemies.
9	It will enable the native to do higher studies. It brings forth positive thinking and makes one an effective decision-maker. If afflicted, danger from speculation, enemies and strangers may occur.

10	If it is a significator of a beneficial House, then success, name, fame, hard work, integrity and gains through government sources. He can be part of the government or administration of public services. Mining might give profits. He will grow with time and age. Initially, the native might have to face many negative things in life. If afflicted, then dishonour, loss of reputation, poverty, and disgrace might strike the individual.
11	It will give lots of material benefits and gains in all endeavours. Will generate support through friends, siblings and peers. Financial gains and promotions are promised if well placed. Success may happen in the Dasa/Bhukthi in litigation. If afflicted, it may lead to many losses, litigation and betrayal. This may lead to strained relations and loss in speculation. There will be a reversal of all those good things we discussed in the previous narrative.

Example Chart 1

	Sun	Mer Ketu	Venus
Moon Asc			Jupiter
Mars	Rasi		
	Rahu Saturn		

Saturn	Mercury	Ketu	Mars
Asc			Jupiter
Moon	Navamsa		
	Rahu Venus	Sun	

The above is a horoscope of a person who started his life in obscurity and poverty. The native had a difficult childhood and could not pursue higher education. In the period of Saturn, at the age of 29, he started an SME (small and medium enterprise), which turned out to be a success. If one observes, we find Saturn is well placed in the 10th House with exalted Rahu. Saturn also has Jupiter's 5th aspect, which is beneficial, being the Lord of the

2nd and 5th and exalted in the horoscope. In Navamsa, Saturn is aspected by a ruling Jupiter, although there are other beneficial effects like Parivarthana Yoga between the 4th and 5th Lord, namely Venus and Mercury. The critical thing to note is that the natives prospered during the Saturn period. Even Adolf Hitler had the 10th House Saturn from Libra ascendant. Though he rose from obscurity to the highest position in Germany, he had to suffer setbacks due to the affliction of the 7th House. We can look at many more charts, but we are limiting it to the discussion of the above charts due to brevity.

Combination

One must remember that Venus, Mercury, and Saturn are complementary. They will do good to each other, and if they are benefics to the native, they will take him to greater heights. Combination with the Sun, Moon, Mars, Jupiter, Rahu and Ketu may not be desirable and might stop an individual's progress in multiple ways. All the above points may come in handy for anyone trying to understand Saturn as a significator of the 6th, 8th, 10th and 12th Houses. One must also remember that Saturn becomes the 10th Lord for the Kalapurusha chart and, therefore, plays a vital role in one's career.

CHAPTER 16

SIGNIFICANCE OF PLANETS AND INCOME

The horoscope is assessed through the planets and the 12 Rasis or Houses. Fundamental issues in life, like education, career, health, income, wealth generation, marriage, etc., are decided on the position of planets and their relation to each other. Each planet signifies a group of affairs and stands for certain outcomes. Jupiter, for example, brings in a happy marriage and excellent children. Venus denotes one's love life and happiness. While reading a horoscope, we can see that the strong planets bring in benefic effects, and the weak planets do not have good effects. Each planet signifies certain walks of life and if they are strong, that part of one's life flourishes. Vedic astrology divides a planet as benefic or malefic. Jupiter, Venus, waxing moon, unafflicted, and Mercury are benefics. Sun, Mars, Saturn, afflicted Mercury and Rahu/Ketu are malefic.

Now, let us see the significance of each planet and their income generating sources:

1. Sun

Sun is our soul and essence of our life. Sun denotes energy, will power and drive. It also represents one's attitude, individuality and the principles he follows in life. Sun gives us the drive to face the challenges in life. Sun should be strongly placed in their birth with required Shadbala for all politicians and people in public life.

Source of Income

Income can be from government services, medicine, mantra initiation, gold, jewellery and grains. It is also karaka for the father and hence inheritance. Money is acquired through self-efforts if the Sun is exalted or in its own house. With a strong Sun, the native may be involved in banking and stock exchange. A weak Sun may lead to obstacles and frustration in life. Sun combination with Saturn is not desirable since it can cause difficulties in one's career or profession. Sun in the 10th house has Digbala and therefore augurs well for career and profession.

2. Moon

The moon is karaka for the mind and mother, basically. It relates to all our emotions, feelings and inner thinking. It represents your attitude and emotional relationship with the spouse. It is feminine in nature and represents white colour. It also refers to one's responsibilities and popularity.

Source of income

They are in the service of royalty or people in higher echelons. Sources of income are the production and marketing of clothes, garments, watery products, chemicals, farming, horticulture, and selling of dairy, fish, snacks, etc. It can represent an author. They get wealth and recognition from the state. They do well in the hospitality industry. They are inclined towards speculation. They can act as a trustee of a public or religious institution. The native with a strong Moon may drive wealth and income through his mother.

3. Mars

Mars is responsible for physical energy and aggressiveness. It indicates a powerful thinking process and related actions. It makes a person individualistic and one with attitude. Mars is instrumental in thoughts of freedom. Mars is related to work; hence, a person with strong Mars can often exhibit controlled aggression.

Source of income

People working in the military, police, security forces, firefighting, sportsmen and sportswomen are all strongly influenced by Mars. Mars can make one a surgeon and a medical practitioner, too. Since it is related to metals, it can make good engineers. Since Mars is Bhumi karaka, it can bring income from real estate and agriculture. The source may be modified depending on other planets' strengths, combinations, and aspects.

4. Mercury

Mercury indicates intellectual abilities, intelligence, quick mind, communication and alertness. Mercury also influences logical and reasoning abilities. It helps one to conceive thoughts and work on them. It indicates expression and writing ability. Strong Mercury induces one to travel.

Source of income

It denotes teaching, speaking, authoring, publication of books and as a successful advocate. Strong Mercury makes one interested in art and architecture. Mercury also represents journalism and income through friends. They may run educational institutions and foundations. They may work in Quasi government and government undertakings.

5. Jupiter

It is a planet of expansion and happiness. It is related to higher learning, especially in religion and philosophy. It relates to luck, achievement and success in all endeavours. Jupiter can make one think abstractly. A weak Jupiter or badly placed Jupiter can make one lazy.

Source of income

The sources of income are legal and religious works, teaching in all spheres, or elder brother. They can be a successful banker if Jupiter is well placed. It can make one a statesman and a politician.

6. Venus

Denotes artistic instincts, beauty, romance, amiability and sociability. Venus enables relationship building, and most successful team leaders have well-placed Venus. It influences one's mind towards art, music and literature. Since it is responsible for a happy married life, it is connected with one's spouse.

Source of income:

Income is generated through gold, gems, jewels, cosmetics, beverages, dairy and animal husbandry. It plays an important role in the hospitality and entertainment industry. Its combination and association with other planets may modify results. It is generally desirable if Venus associates with Mercury and Saturn.

7. Saturn

It is related to hard work, industrious nature, self-discipline, responsibility and limitations. It gives a practical outlook to life. If Saturn is well placed in the chart, it makes one self-made, prudent and with a pragmatic outlook.

Source of income

Money is earned through the government, politics, serving the masses, public undertaking, etc. Income is also generated through mining and metallurgy.

Saturn in 10th without benefic aspect may spell disaster. Affliction with Rahu may mean low-level menial jobs. Saturn, if aspected by the moon and Jupiter, may lead one to the manufacturing industry.

When there is a combination of two more planets, then the nature of occupation and sources of income will be modified. Income and professional success also depend on Dasa/Bhukthi and the transit of planets.

BLURB

*V*edic astrology is an eternal knowledge which is always relevant and beneficial to humanity. *Is Career a Choice* is a book which will answer some of the questions anyone has regarding their career options and what they aim to achieve.

The book explores various aspects related to the profession of Vedic astrology. Particular references to the 10th house, Varga charts, timing in the profession, combination of planets and excerpts from classical texts have been made. Four chapters discuss a combination of planets for various professions. Several charts are discussed with relevance to the profession after careful studies. There is an interesting commentary from classical text in the form of excerpts. The importance of Asthakavarga has been delineated in a short form with examples. A note on Karaka based on the Kalapurusha chart is also appended.

Though short and crisp, the book is exhaustive enough for both astrology students and those conversant with astrology.

www.ingramcontent.com/pod-product-compliance
Lightning Source LLC
LaVergne TN
LVHW041843070526
838199LV00045BA/1415